AF559895

Economic Thought of Mahatma Gandhi

Dr. M. Maharajan
M.A., Ph.D.

School of Gandhian Thought and Development Studies
Mahatma Gandhi University
Kottayam — 686560 (Kerala)

DISCOVERY PUBLISHING HOUSE
NEW DELHI—110 002

Published by :

Discovery Publishing House
4831/24, Ansari Road, Prahlad Street
Darya Ganj, New Delhi—110 002 (INDIA)
Phone : 327 92 45
Fax : 91-11-3253475

First Published—1998

Reprinted-2011

ISBN 81-7141-415-X

Laser Typeset by :

Allied Computers,
Karnal (Haryana)

Printed at :

Mehra Offset Press
Delhi

Preface

The purpose of this study is to analyse how far Gandhian Economic Thought is relevant to contemporary India.

Whole of the world has reached the point of crises today. Poverty, mass unemployment, inflation, environmental pollution and the insecurity of under developed countries are prevailing. Not only the under developed countries but the capitalistic advanced countries have also not been able to eradicate the poverty. The environmental pollution has posed a threat to the health and sanitary conditions and has increased the social cost of production. People are running out of patience and are looking for a system that is alternative for both socialism and capitalism.

The experiment with the democratic-socialistic system, as in India, has proved to be disastrous. The idea behind this was to benefit from the merits of both the capitalism and socialism. But what we have got is the evils of both the system. Bureaucracy, Red tapism, unnecessary controls by the state, mass-poverty, great economic inequalities and unbalanced growth are a few to cite. So what is needed is a system that provides both bread and freedom to the man who is both an individual and a social man. This system should be free of the evils of capitalism and socialism. And Gandhi's economic thought i.e., the concept of 'Trusteeship only can provide such a system. It only can show the wayout of the state of fix the world is in.

Various political scientist, economists, sociologists and spiritualists have studied Gandhi's political, economic, social, religious and spiritual concepts. Some of these scholars are of the view that

Gandhi's ideas are pragmatic and always relevant with some modifications, irrespective of the time and place. But to some others, Gandhi's ideas are entirely irrelevant and inapplicable in an age of scientific and technological progress with its attendant complexity of issues. Whatever may be the contrary views in this on going debate on Gandhism, one thing is beyond doubt that Gandhism presents a new, dynamic, revolutionary and rational approach to existing political and socio-economic problems. Shriman Narayan says that "the more I think about diverse problems facing India at present, the more I feel convinced that Gandhian approach alone will be able to solve, our difficulties on a lasting basis".

In the first chapter an attempt is made to trace the early glimmerings on Gandhi. To understand correctly how Gandhi's mind was moulded one has to go back to his childhood and see what ideas and impressions influenced him most. The influences of childhood generally make a deeper impression and more permanent. Very often they form a focus around which later impressions are grouped. As a boy Gandhi admired the "practiability of his father" but he was greatly influenced by his mother's 'saintliness' and her "deeper religious" nature which later helped him to possess are unquenchable faith in God and made his life a lesson for all ages to come. Gandhi was greatly influenced by the life and teachings of Swami Vivekananda.

The purpose of second chapter is to outline the economic system which Gandhi (and his followers) visualised for India, and to subject the economic ideas embodied in Gandhi's economic system to a close scrutiny.

In the third chapter the primary purpose is to attempt a systematic exposition of the doctrine of growth and the doctrine of employment as a set of ideas and an exposure to an alternative system of thought, compared to conventional macroeconomics.

In the fourth chapter an attempt is made to analyse Gandhi's concept of trusteeship in a frutiful and creative manner.

The fifth chapter deals with Gandhi's concept of decentralisation of economic and political power. His concept of decentralisation is the product of his wide ranging mind which probed into the harsh realities of man's social, political and economic life. From a wider perspective it can be said that Gandhi through his concept of decentralisation was trying to find solutions to certain basic issues like arbitrary state power, unlimited violence, economic exploitation of man by man, removal of poverty and socio-economic inequalities.

In the sixth chapter an attempt is made to assess the prospects of change in the present socio-economic structure of rural areas on Gandhian path of rural industrialisation.

The discussion in the seventh chapter will do no more than touching a few basic issues relating to the relevance of Gandhian economic ideas in the context of Indian planning and will try to enquire into the causes of the present miserable state of affairs of the weaker sections of the population, living particularly in rural areas, inspite of the concreted efforts made under different plans since the very inception of planning in India, adopting the concept of mixed economy, supported by huge plan outlays modern production technology along with the noble objective to initiate a process of development which will raise the living standards and open out to the people new opportunities for a richer and more varied life. This chapter also intends to make out an inner search into the different plans for the purpose to locate the Gandhian content in Indian economic planning and the position of their implementation with intentions and seriousness of the planners and the executors.

In the concluding chapter some of the vital questions are put forth :

a) Have we ever thought to develop our society on Gandhian lines ?

b) Are we really moving in that direction ?

c) Are we thinking on those lines and trying to help the masses ?

d) Are our leaders or rulers leading us in that direction ?

e) Do we have equality of opportunity available to all the countrymen ?

f) Are the rich class of the society or businessmen following the concept of trusteeship in practice ?

g) Do we find morality, virtues, good values etc., being practicised by us and are they reigning supreme over the vices and sins ?

h) Do we have that kind of economic thinking or policies as were advocated by Gandhiji which would have been most beneficial for the teeming masses living in poverty?

If we think deeply and look at the socio-economic structure of our society, we would infact, not get the answers to the above questions in the affirmative. If the Gandhian approach for the development of economy on a decentralised way is adopted, it would also need a change in the present system of education and training. Much of the cost of education and training would be reduced considerably and would not go waste as we find it today. Crores of students are wasting their time, energy and money for getting a kind of education which they find to be quite useless. This has been causing great anxiety and furstration for them. Gandhi's challenge still continues and have some relevance in the welter of the modern technological civilization. Gandhian approach to economic problems has been misunderstood, by many. If human power is properly channelled for constructive purposes, India with her huge man power will one day become the most prosperous and developed nation. At present a vast reserve of human skills and energies, is going to waste. With a little more encouragement, and proper direction by the Government, these energies could provide a dynamic force for India's national development. Therefore we can conclude that Gandhian economic thought may be described as *Pragmatic humanistic economy* because it is based on realistic approach to life with emphasis on human value and human dignity. As Pandit Jawaharlal Nehru rightly put it : "Gandhi is the link between all the past and all the future revolutions of India".

There remains for me a pleasant duty of acknowledgements. My thanks are due to Dr. M. Naganathan, M.A., Ph.D. Professor and Head of the Department of Economics, University of Madras, who allowed me to do research on Gandhian Thought. He was kind enough to provide all opportunities and facilities to continue my research.

I am also very thankful to the controller of examinations Dr. A. Sivamurthy, Ph.D. who permitted me to submit my thesis for the award of D. Litt. Degree University of Madras. I also thank the other concerned authorities of the University of Madras who were sincere enough to provide me with all the facilities.

I hope that this book will prove to be useful for study and research, but even more than it will serve to stimulate further research on Gandhian thought.

I thankfully, acknowledge the help given to me by the Librarian and other staff of the Madras University.

Dr. M. Maharajan

Contents

1
Early Glimmerings and Influences

To understand correctly how Gandhi's mind was moulded one has to go back to his childhood and see what ideas and impressions influenced him most. The influences of childhood generally make a deeper impression and are more permanent. Very often they form a focus around which later impressions are grouped.

Mohandas Karamchand Gandhi was born on the 2nd October 1869 at Porbandar in a coastal city northwest of Bombay, in family belonging to the Bani division of the third ranking Vaisyas. Being born in coastal city within the sound of sea, a certain mysticism had perhaps entered Gandhi's composition-a mysticism which, in later life, linked with a vivid practical sense to make the most formidable of all combinations. His home life was cultured and the family, by Indian standards, was well-to-do. As a boy he admired the 'practicality of his father's but he loved his mother Putli Bai and was greatly influenced by her 'saint liness' and her 'deeply religious' nature which later helped him to possess an unquenchable faith in God and made his life a lesson for all ages to come. It was during him maiden visit to South Africa that Gandhi became conscious of a life mission and throughout his life thereafter he made it his sole concern to be devoted to that mission which was to champion the cause of the victimized and the oppressed as against insolence and might of those who enslaved and oppressed them.[1] Gandhi struggled hard to wipe off racialism that was widely prevalent here. His non-violent struggle against social discrimination strengthened the basic philosophy of life.

It is well-known that Gandhi's life was greatly influenced by his contacts with Leo Tolstoy. Gandhi came to know Tolstoy through 'The Kingdom of God is within you' and his essay on 'Christianity and Patriotism'. The name of the first volume is the Gospel of its author.

Tolstoy's simplicity of life and purity of purpose influenced Gandhi very much. His views on Christianity, its Church, its teachings roused Gandhi's feelings. No profession Christian will disagree with Tolstoy's main contention that must 'die to live' nor fail to be stimulated by the vigour and sincerity with which he restates and elaborates these words of Jesus Christ to suit the exigencies of his day. His famous book "My Confession" followed by 'Criticism of Dogmatic Theology', 'What I believe' and such works reveal his spiritual conflicts and experiences. He came to consider the 'organized' church as the greatest enemy of true Christianity, and found a profound human meaning in Christ's 'Sermon on the Mount' where, among the fine preachings, he laid special emphasis on "Do not resist evil by force'.

Tolstoy accepted love to be the law of life, it was his ambition to revive this law of low and to go back to a simple life of peace and equality. He was so much critical of western countries because they, in their practical life, violated the law of love which was preached by Jesus. The principles of non-violence is based on love for the entire mankind. Both Tolstoy and Gandhi adopted the instrument of love to solve all problems in their lives. 'Love', says Tolstoy, "is the aspiration for communion and solidarity with other souls, and that aspiration always liberates the sources of noble activities. That love is the supreme and unique law of human life, which everyone feels in the depth of one's soul[2]. In his celebrated book 'The Kingdom of God is within you', we find a political force creating an indelible mark on Gandhi. Gandhi confessed that its reading cured him of the scepticism and made him a firm believer of ahiṁsā. Tolstoy and Gandhi firmly believed that non-violence can cure all social maladies, remove political ills, and establish peace on earth and goodwill among mankind. Gandhi says, 'Ahiṁsā, truly understood, is in my humble opinion a panacea for all evils mundane and extra mundane, ... Mahāvirā and Buddha were soldiers, and so was Tolstoy. Only, they say deeper and truer into their profession and found the secret of a time, happy, honourable.and godly life. Let us be joint sharers with those teachers, and this land of ours will once more be the abode of gods[3]. Thus we find that both Tolstoy and Gandhi believed in the efficacy of love and non-violence and Gandhi grasped the essence of these virtues and lead his life directed towards these paths.

It was Tolstoy who impressed upon Gandhi's mind the importance of Bread Labour. For Tolstoy, the man who abstains from manual labour is a thief of the society. Gandhi acknowledged his debt to Tolstoy. He says, 'The Law, that to live man must work, first came home to me upon reading Tolstoy's writing, 'On Bread Labour'............Only those men deserve to eat bread who actually till the ground, spin cloth and produce things'. Tolstoy says, 'Let us get off the shoulder of our neighbors and Gandhi adds that if everyone performed that simple operation, he would have rendered all served God requires of him. Since every man has an obligation to society and to oneself, bread-labour becomes an imperative duty which must be performed by each and every man.

Tolstoy strongly preached against the assumption of Darwinism, Ecclesiasticism and contemporary science and art and he preached a return to the simple innocence of the teachings of the gospels. In his interpretation of the trends and foundations of contemporary civilisations, Gandhi was greatly influenced by Tolstoy. Gandhi's moral and spiritual approach to the problem of Indian civilisation and his quest for spiritual Teleology in the world resulted in his bitter disillusionment of western civilisation. In common with Rousseau and Tolstoy, Gandhi's attitude to Western civilization was moral and philosophical rather than sociological and scientific.

Tolstoy's philosophical anarchism inspired Gandhi much. The ideal society, according to Gandhi is the stateless society, society of enlightened anarchy where social life has become so perfect as to be self-regulated. The pure ideal of Gandhi is an ideal of philosophical anarchism, a stateless, classless society marked by voluntary co-operation. Tolstoy's view bears close resemblance to the Gandhian ideal. He placed his immense faith in the moral development of the people as a final solution to what he considered as the universal oppression of the many by the view. For Tolstoy, the progressive march towards a classless and stateless condition of making depended upon the moral stability and perfection of each individual through observance of the supreme law of love and the consequent repudiation of every form of violence. Profound faith in God, commiseration from the exploited, inherent aversion to violence, deep-rooted belief in the dignity of man led the two philosophers to the same goal. Gandhian ideal, therefore, comes very close to Tolstoyan anarchism.

Gandhi is, however, not a thorough-going Tolstoyan. The difference between the two philosophers arises out of the fact that Gandhi is far more practical than Tolstoy. While Tolstoy in his later life became more or less a recluse far removed from the social and political struggles of his country, Gandhi resolutely championed for the freedom of his country and moral uplift. Gandhi, therefore is essentially a practical idealist. He was not a visionary. Life, no doubt, basically involves some amount of violence. Tolstoy, however, recoils from all expressions of violence. Gandhi permitted violence, provided of course, that the motive for violence was not anger but true love. Thus the moral content of Gandhi's doctrine of ahimsã is of higher significance than that of Tolstoy's. This is due to the fact that Gandhi was greatly influenced by the Gitã ideal of niskãmakarma, i.e., action without attachment.

In short, the Tolstoy Farm of Gandhi is a living monument to Tolstoy. It was not merely a shelter and source of living to the satyãgrahis is South Africa, it stood for the principles that prompted Gandhi and his fellow satyãgrahis to fight for justice. We cannot forget the fact that the technique of satyagraha was cradled and perfected in Tolstoy's concept of non-violence. ' The spontaneous recognition and spiritual collaboration of these two representative men of the accident and the orient's observes Dr. Kalidas Nag, 'have some enduring lessons for our generation, grouping pathetically for some way out of the suffocating gloom of poison gas and mass-slaughter. Whether we shall succeed or not in stopping the fatal march towards another global war, we cannot help hoping for survival in a new world order. We naturally derive the greatest support and consolation from the thoughts and actions of a Tolstoy and a Gandhi who symbolized sanity in a quasi insane world and vicarious sacrifice for the benefit of mankind'[4]. As Ernest J. Simmons observes: 'Thought Tolstoy's beliefs, derived primarily from the teachings of Christianity, have so often been dismissed as of no consequence precisely by the Christian West, they are much alive in the non-Christian East, especially in India, where the mass movement of Sarvodaya aims at the creation of a social order based on the Tolstoyan principle of love inspired by non-resistance or non-violence[5].

Another western philosopher with whom Gandhi felt spiritual brotherhood was he American pacifist Thoreau (1817-1862) who was the champion of the free spirit and was repelled by established political and economic routine of the time. In him we discover an element of moral individualism culminating in his concept of 'Civil Disobedience'. He was a rebel and he challenged the basis of the state in the name of reason and wisdom. Thoreau described civil disobedience in the same terms as Gandhi understood it. He was an anarchist who refused to pay his taxes as a protest against slavery in America. Thoreau used the term 'Civil Disobedience' in one of his speeches in 1849. It is clear that Gandhi did not derive his idea of 'Civil Disobedience', from the writings of Thoreau. In fact, the resistance to authority in South Africa preceded before Gandhi got the essay of Thoreau on 'Civil Disobedience'. This movement was then known as 'passive Resistance.' Gandhi was not satisfied with the term 'Civil Disobedience' because it failed to convey the full meaning of the struggle. Hence he adopted the phrase 'Civil Resistance'.

It is significant that Gandhi drew his inspiration from the works of Thoreau, for Thoreaus was deeply indebted to the East. He did not believe in narrow sectarianism and felt that man was meant to experience God, not to theologies about him. In short, Thoreau sought for his fellowmen a fuller and more natural realization of the self. He once said" 'To the Philosophers, all sects, all nations, are alike. I believe Brahma, Hari, Buddha, the Great spirit, as well God'.

Man, according to Thoreau was a social being who is generally disposed to co-operation with fellow beings for social good. He felt a that the immoral institutions of the state supported by coercive authority hampered the individual's moral and spiritual freedom. He, therefore, visualized a society in which government will disappear. 'That government is best which governs not at all', or at least 'which governs least'[6]. Like Thoreau, Gandhi also held that the democracy can be realised only in a stateless society. It is only in such a society that an individual can have full liberties and enjoy utmost freedom, socially and spiritually. Such a society can be organised on the basis of Truth and Non-violence. A society organised on love and non-violence would equalise the ambitions of men by eliciting the spiritual or divine instinct in man and suppressing the irrational element in it. The ideal society is characterised by a respect of individual liberty and free growth and simultaneous respect for the needs, efficiency, solidarity, natural growth and perfection of the corporate being, the society or nation. Thus Gandhi heard an echo of his own though in Thoreau.

The Gandhian philosophy of Sarvodaya can be traced to the fundamental teaching of India's spiritual heritage although Gandhi had immediate inspiration from Ruskin's Unto This Last of which the term Sarvodaya is his rendering[7]. Sarvodaya (sarva and udaya i.e., rise or welfare of all) has been the basic ideas of Gandhi's philosophy right from the days when he wrote in Gujarati his famous 30,000 word book 'Hind Swaraj' or Indian Home Rule in 1909. Gandhi called one of the chapters of his autobiography 'The Magic Spell of a Book' where in he describes the effects of Ruskin's Unto This Last (Meaning uplift of the last). He translated it later into Gujarati calling it Sarvodaya (meaning the rise or welfare of all). It is a book that gripped the imagination of the great man and he was determined to change his life in accordance with the ideals of the book.

The essential teachings of Ruskin in his original book Unto This Last are than 'men can be happy only if they obey the moral law'. He tells us how men in various walks of life should behave if they intend to translate these ideas into action. Says Ruskin: 'Five great intellectual professions exist in every civilized nation : The soldier's profession to defend it, the pastor's to teach it, the physician to keep it in health, the lawyer's to enforce justice in it, and the merchant to provide for it. The duty of all these men is on due occasion to die for it. For truly, the mean who does not know when to die does not know how to live. Socrates in Plato's Apology gives us similar ideas of the duty of men in various walks of life. Gandhi felt that Ruskins Unto This Last was an expression of Socrate's ideas. Ruskin suggests that man should not run after greater and higher fortunes. Simple pleasure and deeper felicity should be his objective instead. Ruskin believed that a great ear in the history of man will dawn when freedom from want becomes a reality in the life of each and every individual. Freedom from want will usher in the Kingdom of God upon earth.

Gandhi believed like Ruskin that the socio-economic organisation that guarantees the well-being of all-, the high and the low, the right and the poor, the strong and the weak, is the only one worth striving for. What is good for all must also be good for each and everyone individually. Gandhi's modification of the concept from 'Welfare of the last (antyodaya) to 'Welfare of all' (sarvodaya) is profoundly significant. It has been pointed out by Sarvodaya thinkers that the service of the neediest should not be at the cost of humanity.

According to Gandhi, the teachings of Unto This Last are : (1) That the good of the individual is contained in the good of all; (2) that lawyer's work has the same value as the barber's in as much as all have the same right of earning of their livelihood from their work; and (3) that a life of labour, i.e., the life of tiller of the soil and the handicraftsman is the life worth living. The first of these, I know. The second I had dimly realized. The third had never occurred to me. Unto This Last made it as clear as daylight for me that the second and the third were contained in the first. I arose with the dawn to reduce these principles to practice[9]. The revolutionary idea of Sarvodaya was born a new on that memorable day., The phoenix Settlement thus came into existence as an experiment in Ruskinian Socialism almost within days after Gandhi had read Ruskin's 'Unto This Last'.

The philosophy of Sarvodaya which aims at the welfare of all should be the objective of one's activity. It there is any parallel to this ideal in the traditions of the West, we find it not in the ethics of altruism, but in the parable of Jesus[10] which inspired Ruskin to give to his book the title 'Unto This Last'.

Ruskin, Gandhi observed in 1932, 'was content to revolutionise his mind but lacked the strength to change his life. Ruskin's Crown of Wild Olives is also one of Gandhi's favorites. As Gandhi read his deepest convictions in the Gitā, so he wove his own notions into Ruskins. These books appealed to him most which were closest to his concept of life and where they deviated he brought them closer by interpreting them. 'It was a habit with me 'Gandhi once wrote, 'to forget what I did not like and to carry out in practice whatever I liked'.

It is necessary to bear in mind the difference between Ruskin and Gandhi. Unlike Gandhi, Ruskin distrusts the populace. His ideal like that of Carlyle, is the rule of the wisest'[11]. Ruskin was no more a Socialist than Carlyle. Ruskin believes not in democracy but in 'the eternal superiority of some men to others, sometimes even of one man to all others and upholds the advisability of appointing such persons or person to guide, to lead or on occasions even to compel and subdue, their inferiors according to their own better knowledge and wiser will'[12]. Thus Gandhi's views are more akin to those of Tolstoy than to those of Ruskin. It is thus clear that Gandhi's antichrematistic tendencies which were born out of his spiritual outlook in life were strengthened by his studies of Tolstoy, Thoreau and Ruskin.

Gandhian thought owes much to the scriptures of Hinduism, Islam, Christianity Buddhism and Jainism. While Gandhi was in England and in South Africa, he made acquaintance with the world religions. They strengthened in him the consciousness of the spiritual aspect of the well-being of man. He read works on Buddhism and studied the Gītā which he regarded as 'the spiritual reference book'. The nineteen verses describing the sthitaprajña -'one with steady wisdom', Gandhi said has been inscribed on the tablet of his heart; 'they contained for me all knowledge that truths they teach are the external verities'. Gandhi referred to the anāsākti-yoga or gospel of disinterested action as having given him a key as it were to the secret of public work and its success. He wrote: 'A public servant has no personal feelings to be considered...... He must be tulya-nidatamasamstutih'[13]. He wrote: 'My life has been full of external tragedies; and if they have not left any visible and indelible effect on me, I owe it to the teaching of the Gita[14]. According to Gandhi self-realization which forms the central teaching of the Gita is against any line of demarcation being drawn between salvation and wordly pursuits and 'that what cannot be followed out in day-to-day practice cannot be called religion'[15]. Further, renunciations is possible only through the observance of non-violence. Religion is not always opposed to material good. Gandhi desired that one should translate religion in one's day-to-day life's activities. In short, religion has to be lived and practised in home as well as in larger political activities of the state.

Significant for the development of Gandhi's premises was his reading of the book-Edwin Arnold's The Light of Asia, a romanticist version of sayings attributed to Buddha. Gandhi propounds the ethical religion and his views are similar with those of Buddha, who taught that ethical life alone helps us to gain salvation. Gandhi's life was a continuous effort to apply the supreme values of truth and life to all spheres of human existence. Buddha wished to steer clear of profitless metaphysical discussion. "Whatever metaphysics we have in Buddhism is not the original dharma but added to it (adidharama)[16]. The same remark holds good in the case of Gandhi also. Once Gandhi suggested that his writings should be cremated with his body, 'What I have done will endure, not what I have said and written'. This is the same as what Buddha said: 'The Tathagata is free from all theories'. The philosophy of Gandhi is a 'practical philosophy' and not theoretical. It is a coherent philosophy of ethical action of the highest order. In this respect there is a remarkable similarity between Buddha and Gandhi. The Buddha, by opening the doors of Nibbāna for all, aimed, quite successfully, a death blow at this social injustice of caste which reduced the people to intellectual slavery. He declared:

> 'Na jacca vasalo hoti-na jacca hoti brahmano
> Kammana vasalo hoti-Kammana hoti brahmano'.

-not by birth but by deed does one become a brahmin or an outcaste. Thereby, the Buddha advocated social reforms based on the equality of man. He exercised friendly feelings towards all, irrespective of class, caste and creed. He was the first to realize man's social and spiritual progress and to judge people more by character than by the accident of birth. Gandhi, like the Buddha believed in the equality of man. He observes: 'Great as the Buddha's contribution to humanity was in restoring God to His eternal place, in my humble opinion, greater still was his contribution to humanity in his exacting regard of all life, be it ever so low'[17]. Gandhi characterised the Buddha as 'a Hindu of Hindus who was saturated with the best that was in Hinduism'[18]. The basic difference, on the other hand, is that while Gandhi developed a social, economic and political philosophy. Buddha developed a philosophy of the individual. Buddha was a jñāna-yogi, Gandhi was a Karma-yogi although later on in the Mahāyāna, social ethics was greatly emphasised.

That Jaina though influenced Gandhi even before Ruskin and Tolstoy is evidence in the writings of Gandhi. In his Autobiography, he mentions that Rajachandra aroused spiritual quest in him[19]. It is universally known that Jaina philosophy accepts and advocates non-violence (ahiṁsā) as the highest ideal of life and as the means of attaining liberations (mokṣa). Right Conduct (Samyak-caritra) which is the most important part of the ethical discipline of Jainism consists mainly of the 'five great vows' (pañca-mahāvrata), of non-injury (ahiṁsā), truthfulness (satya), non-stealing (asteya), celibacy (brahmacharya) and renunciation (aparigraha); and of these vows, (ahiṁsā) i.e., abstinence from all injury to life, occupies the central place. Influenced to some extent by jaina thought, Gandhi singled out ahiṁsā as the fundamental moral virtue which out to be practised at all times by all men. Gandhi was the first to apply the concept of ahiṁsā to practical life. His sole purpose was to spiritualize secular life.

Albert Scheweitzer and several other Christian interpreters of Gandhian thought consider the emphasis on social service to be indicative of Christian influence on Gandhi. It should, however, be noted that the old Mahāyāna concept of Mahākaruna was imbibed by Gandhi. In his emphasis that service to living beings results in God-realization (moksa), Gandhi attempts to give a modern realistic interpretation of the above concept of Mahākaruna. He is attempting in a sense, to concretize at social and political levels the ideals of Bodhisattva. His ideals, thus, is extension of that Maitreya. He is not content with only the form of a pure and good will but wants to fulfil that moral will with the contents of humanitarian duties and altruistic virtues.

The principle of non-violence which forms the crux of Gandhian thought was also advocated by Patanjali in his yoga-sūtra, which did influence Gandhi. Patañjali reveals the means of non-violence in one of the Sutras by declaring that hatred disappears as soon as non-violence reaches perfection in the yogi. It takes the form of positive love for all creation[20]. Patañjali whose Yogasūtra Gandhi studied in 1903 at Johanesburg included ahiṁsā in his pañcayamas, i.e., the five cardinal disciplines which have since had the pride of place in the Hindu technique of spiritual progress. Patañajali lays down that ahiṁsā is not merely a negative doctrine in the sense of avoidance of violence; it also involves good will towards all creatures. Referring to the five cardinal vows of Patañjali, Gandhi says, It is not possible to isolate any of these in practice. It may be posited in the case of Truth, because it really includes the other four[21]. Gandhi elaborated these yamas and made them an integral part of the discipline of the satyagrahi.

Vaisnavism, the family religion, was the earliest influence on Gandhi during his boyhood days. The Vaisnava doctrine of ahiṁsā and love can, therefore, be regarded as the basis of his philosophy of ahiṁsā. As he grew up, other influence clarified his faith and confirmed him in his deep-rooted conviction. Narasimha Mehta, the friend of the 'untouchables' and composer of Gandhi's favourite hymn-Vaishnava Jana to Tene Kahiye (He is the true Vaishnava etc), which he had sung to Gandhi at every important occassion in his life, inspired him to some extent. But Gandhi did not believe in narrow sectarianism. In fact, his implicit faith in Truth as God and deeper roots in his life than his belief in any sect. Gandhi wrote: 'That hymn-' Vaishnava Jana to Tene Kahiye' is enough to sustain me, even if I were to forget the Bhagavadgītā. To tell you the truth, however, there is one thing which is even simpler but which may possibly be difficult for you to understand. But that has been my pole star all along during life's Journey-the conviction that Truth is God and untruth a denial of Him[22]. After reading Arnold's Light of Asia, he declared that the life of Jesus was similar to that of Buddha. he observed: 'Look at Gautma's compassion;" It was not confined to mankind, it was extended to all living beings[23]. Thus Gandhi inherited the essential principles of Buddhism and Vaisnavism.

During his stay in England, Gandhi was greatly influenced by the writings of the theosophists. Gandhi had the privilege of being introduced not only to Madame Blavatsky (whose key to Theosophy he read) but also to Bernard Shaw's friend Mrs. Annie Besant in London. The key to Theosophy Gandhi wrote" 'Stimulated in me the desire to read books on Hinduism and disabused me of the notion fostered by the missionaries that Hinduism was rife with superstitions[24]. Gandhi refused to join Britain's new theosophist movement, but he rejoined in Mrs. Besant's renunciation and Godliness. Nevertheless, Mrs. Besant's 'How I became a Theosophist' interested him.

A visit to a German Trappist monastery near Durban in 1895 showed him the principles of renunciation, humility and racial respect in practice. So did his conversations with Quakers and missionaries. To the Quakers pacifism and non-resistence have for their basis the fundamental belief that each man's life is guided by an inner light which transcends even the Bible and which rules out my right to constrain men.[25] The Gospel of Quakers is to spiritualise politics, freeing it of all violence and conducting the state on non-violent lines. But this movement is entirely different from Gandhian conception of Satyāgraha. A full account of the birth of Satyāgraha was given by Gandhi himself in the 12th Chapter of his book Satyāgraha in South Africa. He has discussed therein the question of the origin of the idea of passive Resistance through the activities of the Quakers, the Non-conformists, the Sufragettes, etc. In many such cases Gandhi detected deviations from strict non-violence. Only in the case of Jesus Christ he accepted his resistence as the pure set form of Satyāgraha 'whose example is few and far between in History'.

Gandhi' attitude to Christianity is different to judge. It has been said that Gandhi 'embraced Christ but rejected Christianity.[26] For Jesus he had abundant reverance, but many aspects of Christianity left him uneasy. 'Much of what passes as Christianity', he once wrote, 'is a negation of the Sermon on the Mount.... Paul was not a Jew. He was a Greek, had an oratorical mind, and he distorted Jesus. Christ Possessed a great force-the Love force- Christianity became disfigured when it came to the West. It became the religion of kings.[27] Nevertheless Gandhi saw the positive side of the Christian faith in England and renewed his study of the Bible. 'Jesus played a great part in my life, ' he said many years later, 'unconsciously how much, I do not know; consciously how much, I do know. When I began to read the Sermon on the Mount, I felt the beauty of it. I cannot say that it is singular, or that it is not to be found in other religions. But the presentation is unique. So many of my words are chosen from the Bible. In my talks I canot avoid reference to the Bible; I am unable to speak without reference to it.[28] Gandhi wrote: 'Though I cannot claim to be a Christian in the sectarian sense, the example of Jesus' suffering is a factor in the composition of my undying faith in non-violence which rules all my actions, wordly and temporal.[29] Dr. Stanley Jones says of Gandhi 'One of the most Christ like men in history was not called a Christian at all[30]. The Sremon on the Mount especially created an indelible impression on his mind. Gandhi's detachment from wordly possession, non-violence, and universal love owe much to this exalted scripture. The life and character of Gandhi is more or less similar to Jesus. The martyrdom of Gandhi was due to his preaching liberalism in religion and universalism in love. The powerful and external teaching of Jesus consists in suffering death in following the righteous path. Satyāgraha is the practical application of the above teachings by Gandhi.

As for Islam, Gandhi declared that in his view 'the point of brotherhood is manifested in no other religion as clearly as in Islam'. As a student in England Gandhi has read the chapter ' The Hero as a Prophet' in Carlyle's 'Heroes and Hero-worship' and learnt of the Prophet's greatness and bravery and austere living. He also read sale's translation of the Koran in the early years of his stay in South Africa. He was encouraged to find that in moments of despair and confusion Mohammad also fasted and prayed. Mohammad's practical instinct as a reformer and his monotheism has been a 'constant strength and support to Gandhi'.[31] At his prayer meetings, verses from the Qurān were invariably chanted along with those from the Gītā and none objected. This was a lesson in tolerance and discipline. Can there be a better follower of Prophet and Jesus than Gandhi ? According to him the chief contribution of Islam has been the brotherhood of man. The common Muslim salutation As-Salamalai Kum means'peace be on you'. 'Many Musalmans', wrote Gandhi, 'will not even allow me to say that Islam, as the word implies is unadulterated peace. My reading of the Koran has convinced me that the basis of Islam is not violence[32]. Gandhi regards Christianity, Buddhism, Islam and Hinduism, as religions of peace. Truely Gandhi practised the essential principles of world religions in his daily life and showed the path of peace to humanity at large. The new-Hinduism of Gandhi has a synthetic unity of these religions. He wrote" 'My young mind tried to unify the teachings of the Gītā, the Light of Asia and the Sermon on the Mount.......I read the chapter on the Hero as a Prophet (Mohammad) and learnt of the Prophet's greatness and bravery and asustere living[33]. Thus Gandhi shows remarkable catholicity and sympathetic and reverential attitude towards all religions of the world. His goal of life was to regenerate moral and social values in the Indian masses, and through them, in the world at large. In Gandhian teachings we find religion and ethics always go together. He wrote: 'There is no such thing as religion over-riding morality.[34] In fact he spiritualised politics by his firm religious convictions which were universal in its nature.

Gandhi imbibed the moral teachings of prophets of Asia, viz., Rāma, Buddha, Mahāvira, Moses, Jesus, Zoraoster, Confucius, Nānak, Vivekānanda, and other prophets, and was content not merely with an inward realization of the moral precepts but wanted to make them dynamic. The revival of the ancient teachings by Gandhi and incorporating them in his philosophy of Sarvodaya is perhaps his greatest contribution to world thought.

To sum up, Gandhi is the child of Indian Renaissance. Schopenhaur regarded Buddha and Christ as the ideal men of history because they had renounced home life and taught abnegation. oswald Spengler, on the other hand, regarded fact and power as more significant elements in history than contemplation and truth. But Gandhi, as one of the epoch-making figures in India, combined both moral idealism and political success. He is a unique figure because of the simple and straight-forward views which he preached and practised without swerving from truth at every moment during his long career as a social reformer, a political teacher, a saint, a true lover of humanity and an apostle of non-violence, truth, love, goodness and peace.

The entire life of Gandhi was a experiment with truth, and the experiment ultimately proved the victory of truth over untruth, of lover over hatred and violence. Anyone who had closely followed the career of Gandhi from the time of his espousing the cause of the Indians in South Africa till the day of his tragic assassination at the hands of his own countrymen and of his own faith will be struck by certain qualities whose combination went to make him tower like Mount Everest above his greatest contemporaries in India and abroad. If there was in him a great deal of the saint there was also in him many of the simple traits of the peasant and the common man.

Gandhi's autobiography, The Story of My Experiments with Truth, that extraordinary human document, is a record of his individual transformation from an ordinary man into an apostle of truth. In his boyhood he read a play sravana-pitrubhaktinātaka. He also saw it enacted. The play created an everlasting impression on his mind. 'Here is an example for you to copy' he said to himself. He also saw the play 'Harischandra'. This play set him on a career of seeking truth.

There was a deep religious background in his life which can be traced to the influence of his mother Putli Bai, whom he adored. Reciting Bhagavadgītā, reading aloud verses from the great Rāmāyana and constant reciting of the hymn by the saint poet Narasimha Mehta 'Vaisnava Janato' led Gandhi to the conviction that morality was the basis of things and truth was the substance of all morality.

References

1. T.M.P. Mahadevan Outlines of Hinduism, op.cit., pp. 78-79.
2. Leo Tolstoy's letter to Mahatma gandhi, dated 7th sept, 1910.
3. Speeches and Writings of Mahatma Gandhi, N.P.H., Ahmedabad, Fourth Edn., p. 384.
4. Kalidas Nag, Tolstoy and Gandhi, Pustak Bhander, Patna, p.121.
5. Ernest, J. Simmons, Leo Tolstoy-Selected Essays, the Modern Library, New York, 1964, p. IX.
6. Henry D. Thoreau, Civil Disobedience, The Civil Art Press, New York, 1952, p.10.
7. Ruskin's Unto This Last was first published in 1862. But it was on 19th March 1904 that Gandhi had the opportunity to read that book when it was given to him by his friend Mr. Polak during his twenty-four hours' journey from Johannesburg to Durban.
8. Ruskin, Unto This Last, N.P.H, Ahmedabad, p.22.
9. Gandhi, Autobiography, N.P.H. Ahmedabad, 1958, part IV, p.22.
10. St, Mathew, Ch. XX, Versus 12-14; According to this parable in St. Mathew, the good house-holder who hired labourers for work in his vineyard paid those who joined later the same wage that he had agreed to pay those who joined early. These labourers who were hired about the eleventh hour received the same wage as those who were hired earlier. When the latter expressed their dissatisfaction saying, 'those last have wrought but one hour, and thou hast made them equal unto us, which have borne the burden and heat of the day', the good man of the house replied answering one of them, and said, 'Friend, I do thee no wrong: dids't not thou agree with me for a penny? Take that thine is, and go thy way: I will give unto this last, even as unto thee'.
11. Gopinath Dhavan, The Political Philosophy of Mahatma Gandhi, N.P.H., Ahmedabad, 1951, p.33.
12. Quoted by E.Barker in 'political Thought from Spencer to today'.

Oxford University Press, p.193 Another similar pasage dispargaging majorities is: 'In every vital moment the right opinion is in the minority of one... See only that you set over every business vital to you, one man of sense, honour and heart,. The works of Ruskin (116 ed.), Vol, XXXI, p.505.

13. M.K. Gandhi, Harijan, 15-12-1933.
14. M.K. Gandhi, Young India, 6-8-1925, p.274.
15. Louis Fischer, The Life of Mahatma Gandhi, Jonathan cape, London, 1957 p.48.
16. S. Raḍhakrishnan , Indian Philosophy, George Allen & Unwin Ltd., London, 1966, Vol.I, p. 353.
17. M.K. Gandhi, Young India, 24-11-1927, pp. 392-393.
18. M.K. Gandhi, All Religions are true, Bombay, 1962, p. 197.
19. See the present writer's 'Non-violence according to Jaina philosophy and Gandhiji technique's, in Bhagya Bharani', Madras, p.48-52.
20. ahiṁsā pratiṣṭāyaṁ tat sannidhau vairātyāgah, patañjali Yoga-sutra Sadhana Pāda 35.
21. D.G. Tendulkar, Mahatma, Vol. VII, 1962, p.292.
22. M.K. Gandhi, Young India, 10-12-1925, pp 431 & 433.
23. Kalidas Nag, Tolstoy and Gandhi, op. cit, p. 34.
24. Ibid,. p. 25.
25. A.C.F. Deales, History of Peace, p. 34.
26. Louis Fischer, The Life of Mahatma Gandhi, op. cit., p. 131.
27. Ibid., p. 132.
28. Quoted from Gandhiji's correspondence with Government, by C.S. Shukla: Gandhi's view of life, p. 189.
29. M.K. Gandhi, Harijan, 7-1-1939, p. 417.
30. S.K. George, Gandhiji's Challenge to Christianity, N.P.H. Ahmedabad, 1947.
31. C.F. Andrew, Mahtma Gandhi's Idea, pp. 63-64.
32. M.K. Gandhi, Harijan, 12-11-1938, p. 327.
33. Ibid, p. 328.
34. M.K. Gandhi, Young India, 24-11-1921, p. 385.

2
Gandhian Economic System : Its Relevance to Contemporary India

The failure of the planning system in India to produce the desired results led to the questioning of the path of development pursued so far in the country as also to the emergence of a number of schools propounding alternative strategies of development. One such school which became rather active particularly in the early '70s and which styled itself as Gandhian described the path of development followed so far in India as "un-Indian and elitist"[1]. This school found in Gandhian thought a path of development which was purported to be purely Indian and oriented to the needs of the masses. The purpose here is to outline the economic system which Gandhi (and his followers) visualised for India, and to subject the economic ideas embodied in Gandhi's economic system to a close scrutiny.

Gandhi *Vs* Gandhians

At the outset it is desirable to clarify one point" that is, the fact of what Gandhi had been talking and what his followers, Gandhians, have been now saying are not identical in all respects. This divergence may be due perhaps to the varying interpretations given to whatever Gandhi wrote and spoke. It may be noted that Gandhi did not produce a treatise or some such thing on the economic system which he visualised for India. In some of his general works, lectures, letters written to, or editorials in, "Young

India" and Harijan he made references to the kind of economic system which according to his was ideal for the country. Those who wrote about Gandhi's economic system pieced these bits of writings together and produced what, according to them, was the kind of economic system that Gandhi had visualised. As interpretations could in any case not be uniform such efforts naturally produced varying models of development attributed to Gandhi. Here it may be worthwhile picking up two strands; one representing Gandhi's critics and the other representing his followers. The former surprisingly used the minimum of interpretation to the writings of Gandhi and the picture projected by them could in fact be regarded as Gandhi's economic system. The latter on the other hand appear to have read too much between the lines and to have produced some sort of a window-dressed picture of the economic system attributed to Gandhi. For convenience of analysis this may be termed as the Gandhian economic system as distinct from the term Gandhi's economic system referred to above[2]. In what follows is presented in two separate sections, Gandhi's Gandhian paths of economic development.

Gandhi's Economic System

Gandhi's economics ideas were in a sense a logical corollary of his political and moral principles such as Swaraj, Sarvodaya, "truth and non-violence" and the like. Based on these wider social principles Gandhi derived his economic ideas which if brought together would give a picture of the economic system that he visualised.

The most important principles which influenced Gandhi, and which later became the guiding spirit behind all his ideas, was the principle of Sarvodaya-the good of all. This principle originated out of his reading of Ruskin's "Unto This Last" which held that the good of individual contained in the good of all. It was Gandhi's desire that the good should percolate even to the last of the socio-economic ladder -the poorest of the poor. Given the goal of Sarvodaya Gandhi was confronted with the question of what kind of economic system the country should evolve for itself. It was in this context that his wider social ideas of swaraj truth and non-violence inspired him to evolve an economic system which was consistent with this political and moral philosophy. From the idea of swaraj emerged the ideas of swadeshi and self-sufficiency. And from the principle of truth and non-violence emerged a series of economic ideas like non-exploitation, non-possession, trusteeship, bread-labour and so on. All these ideas, which in fact having originated under different contexts, formed the founding pillars of Gandhi's economic system.

Gandhi believed that the economic good of all lay in adopting the principle of swadeshi or self-sufficiency. Though Gandhi used the principle of swadeshi earlier as a political weapon to boycott the foreign goods, particularly of the British, it actually acquired economic overtones gradually. It would be noted that the concept of swadeshi inculcated gradually in the minds of Indians the imperative and the value of self-sufficiency both at the national and at the local village level. He later used this concept along with the other economic idea viz., decentralisation, as a technique of building an economic system which was purely Indian and mass based.

His belief that India lived in villages led him to propound the concept of village swaraj which, among other things, envisaged village self-sufficiency. In its extreme form, village self-sufficiency not merely meant non-dependence of the village on other villages for its economic needs but it also meant self-sufficiency among households. This meant that each household would produce its own requirements-food, clothing and other things-and never depend on others for its economic needs.

The justification for village self-sufficiency originates from his ideas of non-exploitation. Gandhi was aware of the evils of the capitalist form of production particularly of its exploitative nature. As he was also aware of the invaluable advantages of personal interest that is associate with the capitalist production he tried to evolve a production system which while retaining the advantage of self-interest eliminated the exploitative mechanism. In this context Gandhi came out with two proposals. The first, which is very widely known and debated, is the concept of trusteeship. As this concept has been widely discussed and is well known it may not be necessary to discuss its implications here. The second proposal which is less known but, in our opinion, appears to be fundamental to Gandhi's economic system in his proposal that a productive system which ensured simultaneity in production and distribution should be evolved. Gandhi believed that the satisfaction of this condition would eliminate the exploitative mechanics of the capitalistic system. It is as a means of attaining a process of production which would cause both production and distribution to take place simultaneously that Gandhi advocated the principle of swadeshi which in essence envisaged the indigenisation of not merely methods and patterns of production but also of the market.

A word now about indigenised methods and patterns of production, and markets and about the manner in which indigenisation would ensure simultaneity in production and distribution. The measure suggested by Gandhi for ensuring production and distribution to take place simultaneously was to orient all productive activities to the satisfaction of the basic needs of the masses. This meant that production pattern should be uni-dimensional confining itself to the basket of necessaries only. The emphasis on basic necessaries is derived from his abhorrence to luxuries which in his opinion are inspired by western societies. When the production pattern aimed at meeting the requirements of the masses it naturally would result in the localisation of production and distribution and when this happened, Gandhi argued, distribution would automatically get regulated. This, he held that if mass production was concentrated in particular areas: "you would have to go about in a round about way to regulate distribution, whereas if there is production and distribution both in the respective areas where things are required, it is automatically regulated, and there is less chance for fraud, none for speculation".[3]

This actually would require that production centres should be dispersed and located at consumption centres to facilitate both production and distribution to take place simultaneously. As a means of ensuring that exploitation did not place Gandhi desired that the methods of production should be indigenised. And as part of this he objected to the use of machines. To quote him: "Machinery has its place; it has come to stay. But it must not be allowed to displace human labour. An improved plough is a good thing. But if by some chances, one man could plough up by some mechanical invention of his the whole of the land of India, and control all the agricultural produce and if the millions had no other occupation, they would starve and being idle, they would become dunces ...."[4]

Therefore, his objection to the use of machine arose on account of its abuses such as labour displacement, and, more importantly, the possibility of the producers growing into monopolists with control over production and distribution. However, what is not clear is the mechanics by which machines caused distribution to be centralised and opened up possibilities of exploitation. One possible explanation could be that: "the use of machines leads to mass production causing concentration of production at one place and distribution centres to be located at far distant places. In the Gandhian system the dissociation of production and distribution is a sufficient condition to generate forces of exploitation. These forces according to Gandhi are fraud and speculation......"[5]

The other possible explanation as given by Bandekar is: "that capital has a tendency to cumulate and concentrate in ever fewer hands. Gandhi's apprehension is that this may lead either to an unlimited and uninhibited pursuit of material wealth and comfort or to a situation in which a few produce all the needs of the society while a large majority is denied opportunity to work and earn their daily needs".[6]

The clear disapproval of use of machines apart there is also disapproval of production of modern goods and amenities. Gandhi held: "India's salvation consists in undoing what she has doing during the past fifty years or so. The railways, telegraphs, hospitals, lawyers, doctors and such like have all to go, and the so-called upper classes have to learn to live consciously and religiously and deliberately the simple life of a peasant knowing it to be a life giving true happiness.......".[7]

Gandhi's disapproval of modern goods and amenities again originates out of his fear that production and distribution of such goods and amenities would sow the seeds of exploitation. Such economic activities deviating from the goal of production simple necessaries of life apart would also create a band of parasites who live on the earnings of the hard working peasants and workers. It is in this context that he propounded his principles of "bread labour" as a measure of forcing everybody to physically work and to earn his livelihood. He used this principles to discourage parasitic living by some sections of the population. J. D. Sethi, a well known Gandhian economist, explains the principle of bread-labour as follows: "Bread-labour in simple terms implied that amount of physical labour, given the arts of production and the society determined necessities, which is required from each person to production these necessities. That much labour time must be spent by everybody in physical labour. Anyone who does not work with his hands or other limbs runs the risk of being a parasite. Even the greatest thinker, poet or philosopher is likely to be misled by his own ideas and plagues of sophistication if he is not involved in some physical action".[8]

To sum up, in Gandhi's economic system one is expected to be self-sufficient-producing one's own requirements and not in the least dependent on others. The goods to be produced and consumed should be basic necessities and there is hardly any room or justification for the production of modern luxuries and amenities. The goods should however be produced by traditional methods, and machine has no place in Gandhi's economic system. Added to this, there is the requirement that each adult member should put in an eight-hour physical labour to earn his daily bread and there is no room for intellectual or mental labour in his economic system. All this is needed to prevent exploitation of man by man. The principle which according to Gandhi would prevent exploitation is the principle of simultaneity of production and distribution.

Thus in Gandhi's system people are expected to live a life of simplicity. This, according to Gandhi, is possible by "self-abnegation and abstermiousness" and by not falling a victim to the charms of modern civilization which lays the trap of expanding material wants. It is this content of Gandhi's economic system that provoked some economists to hold that this system was not relevant to us in the present context. A representative view on this may be quoted here:"...... the Gandhian Path is not an alternative path of reaching the same goal of economic development which the country has pursued in the past 45 years. It is a path leading to an alternative goal of human life and existence; a human society which is unmoved and immovable, unchanged and unchangeable using the same kind of plough as existed a thousand years ago, living in the same kind of cottages as there were in times immemorial and educating its people on the same system as ever before; a society which limits and minimises its material needs and one in which every one earns his daily bread by a full day's physical labour seeking happiness as a mental condition detached from the objective material conditions of life. I shall not say that goal is necessarily utopian. I have a simpler point, namely that the Gandhian goal is not acceptable. If one is talking in the name of the common men and trying to meet his aspirations, it is important to recognise that Gandhian goal is not relevant. What is equally important and must be explicitly recognised is that the Gandhi path does not lead to the goal which today is relevant".[9]

Gandhian Economic System

The attack on Gandhi's economic system as being irrelevant to contemporary development problems has led to attempts of reviving Gandhism couched in modern theories of development and planning. Such a revival required selection of Gandhi's pronouncements which related to development strategies and translation of these into the vocabulary of contemporary development analysis. The Gandhians-the followers of Gandhian philosophy did this.[10]

Looking at the Indian Planning experience since the '50s the Gandhians held that the planners made two kinds of errors in economic resource mobilisation and allocation. These errors are—(1) the attempts to technically modernise the Indian economy faster than the conditions of the economy would permit, and (2) the attempt to use international trade mechanism in an 'accumulationist' fashion, thereby increasing the capital-intensity of the investment-mix. These errors, having originated from the faith in the modern economic growth, obviously led to structural unemployment and mass poverty in the country. The faith in modern economic growth characterized by high investment mix originated out of the elites' desire to remain part of the international capitalistic economic system. The desire to remain part of such a system compels the decision-makers to succumb to international compulsions such as (1) high technological development in the export sector to keep exports growing, (2) technological compulsions implicit in the structure of imports, (3) consumption pattern compulsions resulting from intentional demonstration effect, and (4) infrastructure development compulsions resulting from the above three factors causing the elites to build modern ports, modern airports, modern cities, hotels and transport and so on.

All these promoted a high capital-mix investment pattern in the economy which is quite inappropriate to the prevailing factor proportions. The eradication of structural unemployment and mass poverty would require opting out of the international capitalistic economic system. This however would not mean that the economy would totally sever its economic relations with the international economy. It only means that there would be some sort of a semi-autarchic pattern where international trade is used only for securing minimum of the trade advantages such that all consumable imports would be import-substituted under labour intensive techniques and only technological capital goods needed for mass employment industries would be imported.

Having outlined the Gandhian diagnosis of the ailment of the Indian economy we may now present in some detail the Gandhian development strategy. The Gandhian development strategy by and large envisages redirection of investment flows towards the more labour intensive sectors. The main concern of the Gandhian is (1) provision of employment opportunities to the growing work force and (2) provision for the future growth of the economy. This requires that the investible resources should be so allocated between the sectors that both, the needed employment opportunities and savings are created. As higher reinvestible surplus and lower employment potential are associated with higher capital intensity, and lower reinvestible surplus and higher employment potential are associated with lower capital intensity, the planner will be called upon to strike at that point of capital intensity which is appropriate for promoting the right rates of employment and savings growth. The whole exercise of arriving at such a point may be illustrated by means of diagram.[11] Axes and x and y respectively measure growth rate of labour demand and growth rate of saving. The negatively sloping transformation frontier, NP, which measures the capital intensity of investible resources is composed of points which represent different combinations of growth rates of labour and growth rates of savings that the economic system could attain for a given level of investible resources. Thus at point N the economy could have OM growth rate of labour demand and MN growth rate of savings. If OE is the rate at which the labour force is growing then EF is the employment growth constraint that the planner has to keep in mind while allocating resources to the economic activities of varying capital-intensity. Similarly, If OS is the minimum savings growth rate that is needed to promote future income growth then SR is the savings growth constraint which the planner has to keep in mind while allocating investible resources. These constraints give the segment AB called the satisfying segment which represents satisfactory choice points of capital intensity. At point A the resource allocation pattern, while absorbing the incremental

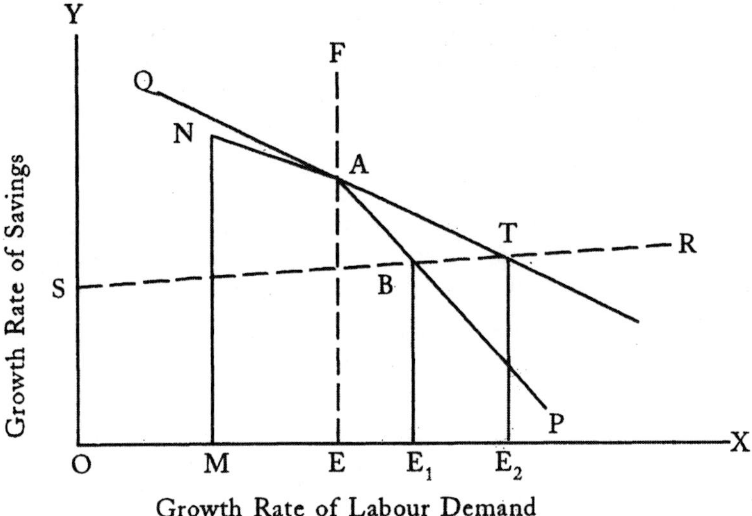

labour force, achieves a higher rate of savings growth which ensures a higher future growth. At point B the resource allocation pattern, while ensuring the desired future growth rate, creates employment opportunities faster than the labour increment can take. The contention of the Gandhians is that at present the developing economies which suffer from mass poverty and structural unemployment, instead of operating along the AB segment for the transformation curve, are operating along the NA segment meaning that their resource allocation pattern is of growth rather than employment preference type.

The analysis presented thus far has been in a closed framework where the influence of foreign trade is taken into account. The Gandhians show that even within the Gandhian framework it is possible to derive advantages from trade with foreign countries. It is their contention that at present the developing economies are following the accumulationist approach in their foreign economic relations. That is, these countries in their anxiety to export capital intensive products follow a capital intensive investment pattern which while cutting on the employment potential actually raises the rate of accumulation through improved savings rates. Thus assume that, as in the above diagram, the economy is in a state of domestic balance in respect of the production of capital intensive and labour intensive sectors at Point A. If the economy tries to expand its export sector by producing and exporting capital intensive products it jumps up and moves along the AQ segment of the new transformation line. This indicates that for every along this line the economy loses in employment potential gains in growth rate of savings giving you a situation of future growth preference over the present employment growth. Gandhians would like to use international trade for accelerating employment potential without sacrificing future income growth potential. There argument is that if the developing economies could obtain capital and intermediate goods cheaper through trade than by domestic production then

(1) there is expansion of the labour-intensive sector as a step to create an export surplus to meet the imports and

(2) also the dangerous possibility of the capital and intermediate goods shortage threatening the economy is removed. The first possibility expands the employment potential and the second ensures that the rate of savings growth is not brought down. To go back to the diagram, let us assume that the economy is in a state of balance in respect of the production of capital intensive and labour intensive sectors at point B where the employment growth rate is OE_1 and savings growth rate is E1B. With the opening of foreign trade the economy moves from point B to Point T where while the savings growth rate continues to be same at E1B, the employment growth rate rises from OE1 to OE2. It is, however, cautioned by the Gandhians that such advantages from trade is possible only if the economy could obtain capital goods from foreign countries cheaper through exchange than by domestic production. If such condition is not obtainable the guideline is that there should be no trade relations with other countries.

Some Observations

Looking closely at the strategy of development suggested by the Gandhians one is relieved to find that this strategy envisages a path for growing rather than a stagnant economy as envisaged by Gandhi. For, in the Gandhian path of development there is room for savings to emerge and capital formation to take place as against a nil net capital formation implied in Gandhi's economic system. Secondly, the Gandhian path of development, though lays emphasis on growth of employment opportunities, also proposes an appropriate rate of savings for future growth of the economy. It may be noted that this appears to have some parallels with Joan Robinson's concept of "Golden Age" which envisages a situation of capital accumulation taking place at a rate that it absorbs the growing labour force of each point of time along the time horizon. In the Gandhian system employment generation is given priority. But the allocation of resources is proposed in manner that growth rate of employment takes place at a rate that it coincides with the desired future growth rate of the economy at different points of time along the horizon. This is the Gandhian "Golden Age" which is Robinsonian Golden Age in reverse. The concept of Gandhian Golden age of great analytical importance to the developing economies which are steeped in poverty and unemployment. It throws up a goal of development which is unquestionably relevant to such economies and gives a set of investment criteria which should guide the planning body in its resource allocation exercises.

A question that one should however ask at this point is how far is the Gandhian strategy of development faithful to the original process of Gandhi. Two points that are implied in the Gandhian path of development make this path quite alien to Gandhi's thought and belief. One of these relates to the investment pattern and the other to foreign trade. To take up the second first, it is doubtful whether Gandhi ever envisaged a growth path which made use of foreign trade either as a growth engine or as an instrument of employment promotion. He was a staunch follower of the principle of swadeshi which shunned even inter-village trade not to speak of international trade. As a matter of fact Gandhi was against foreign trade not because he hated foreign political domination but because he thought that foreign trade was responsible for the decline of the flourishing cottage and small-scale industries. In the circumstance, it would be difficult to believe that Gandhi would have permitted foreign trade in his economic system even assuming that it promised some benefits. Coming to the first point, it may be noted that the pattern of investment preferred by Gandhi was such that it not merely produced essential consumer goods but also attained simultaneity in production and distribution. The letter condition, as we have seen, was achievable only where the production and consumption centres were not divorced from other. In other words, in Gandhi's system each household produced its own requirements with simple tools and implements and never, perhaps, thought of exchange as that would bring in possibilities of exploitation. The

Gandhian path of development on the other hand appears to be deviating from Gandhi's laudable goal of non-exploitative economic system. The Gandhian model of development, it may be noted, envisages investment allocation to sectors of varying capital intensity in a manner that it ensures both full employment and growth. Though the model prefers low capital intensive projects in general it seeks to divert a portion of the resources to high capital intensive projects with a view to ensuring high savings rate and future growth. This by itself is anti-Gandhi as according to Gandhi the capital intensive machine using methods of production sow the seeds of exploitation. It is thus evident that the Gandhian model actually violates some of Gandhi's basic principles and as one reads along the Gandhian literature that is coming out now a days one would not help wondering whether Gandhi ever spoke or stood for all that is attributed to him.

References

1. See Jayaprakash Narayanan's foreword to J.D. Sethi, Gandhi Today, (New Delhi: Vikas Publishing House, 1978), p.viii.
2. One writer uses the terminologies of "classical Gandhism" and "new-Gandhism" in place of our " Gandhism" and "Gandhianism". See Das A. Foundations of Gandhian Economics, (Bombay Allied publishers, 1979).
3. Harijan, 2.11.1934.
4. Young India, 5.11.1925.
5. Abdul Aziz, "The Gandhian Path of Industrialisation: Some Questions". a paper submitted to the seminar organised by the Gandhi Foundation, Allahabad University, Allahabad.
6. V.M. Dandekar, "Gandhian Economic System: A path of Non-economic Goals" in B.C. Das and G.P. Mishra, Gandhi in Today's India, (New Dehi, Ashish Publishing House, 1979) p.84.
7. See N.K. Bose, Selection, from Gandhi (Ahmedabad, Navajivan publishing House, 1948).
8. J.D. Sethi, Gandhi Today, Op. cit., p. 36.
9. V.M. Dandekar, "Gandhian Economic System: A path to Non-economic Goals", Op. cit., pp. 91-2.
10. See Das, A Foundation of Gandhian Economics, Op. Cit., P. viii.
11. The diagram given here is derived from a series of diagram presented by Das A. in his Foundations of Gandhian Economics, op. cit.

3
The Economics of Growth and Employment : The Gandhian Approach

In modern macroeconomics, growth and employment are two of the major areas of concern, from the point of view of economic theory as well as policy. At the theoretical level, growth poses certain questions. What leads to growth? What are the preconditions of growth? What are the limits on growth? Under what conditions can balanced growth be achieved? At the policy level, the attention if focused on strategies designed to accomplish specified growth objectives. Reliance is placed on public policies to influence the development of resources and technology. The meaning of growth of more or less, taken for granted, that is to say that growth is part of economic dynamics economics of employment, on the other hand, can be either static or dynamic depending on how one treats the element of time. In its static form, economic theory deals primarily with the determinants of employment, with given resources, and with given technology. In its dynamic form, it is theoretical inquiry into the process of change over time. It becomes an integral part of the economics of growth and therefore, a part of economics. In macroeconomics, it is important to recognize this link between growth and employment. It is especially important in a discussion of the economics of growth and employment from the Gandhian perspective.

Gandhi did not construct a formal theoretical system which can be characterized, strictly speaking, as macroeconomics. It is understandable because he had neither any formal training in pure economics nor any interest in building and purely theoretical system. From his voluminous writings, however, it is not too difficult to deduce certain macroeconomics doctrines relating particularly to the central issues of growth and employment. These doctrines may be lacking in the underpinnings of a rigorous economic theory but not in the power to challenge conventional macroeconomic thinking. Perhaps this is what accounts for the inherent vitality of the Gandhian doctrines. Being an untrained economist was perhaps an intellectual advantage rather than an intellectual handicap for Gandhi. It gave him the freedom, ordinarily unavailable to a professional economist, to go beyond the narrowly defined limits of pure economics and raise issues which are highly pertinent and yet are generally overlooked in conventional economics of growth and employment. By doing so, Gandhi was able to force us to think that economic issues are multidimensional and hence it is not sufficient to be aware of only one dimension. Gandhi's methodology of economic analysis appears to have a great deal of merit, even though the particular doctrines that Gandhi formulated on the basis of the methodology may be found unacceptable or unworkable in a particular society and at a particular stage of history. One can hardly be-little its importance as "an apparatus of the mind". For an understanding of the economics of growth an employment from the Gandhian perspective, it is essential to familiarize oneself with the background of his system of thought.

First, one must note that the Gandhian doctrines were enunciated in the context of the peculiarities of the Indian economy and, therefore, they may not be generalizable. Economic stagnation, massive poverty, urban industrialization coupled with rural de-industrialization, large-scale rural unemployment and under employment, gross inequality of income distribution heavy dependence of rural population on urban industries, concentration of industrial power and productive capacity in urban centres, heavy reliance on imported, large-scale technology, and inter-sectoral imbalance reflected in urban affluence and rural poverty are some of the important characteristics of the Indian economy that influenced that orientation of the Gandhian doctrines of growth and employment.

Second, one must keep it in mind that Gandhian doctrines-economic, or political, or social-cannot be fully understood out of context of his broader philosophical system. He built this system on the cornerstones of two fundamental philosophical concepts: truth and non-violence. It is, therefore, understandable why an essentially moral approach towards the individual and society pervades through all the Gandhian doctrines, his doctrines of growth and employment being no exception. It was impossible for him to offer an economic doctrine that did not embody his moral philosophy. In his own words, "Economics is untrue which disregards moral values. The extension of the law of non-violence in the domain of economics means nothing less than the introduction of moral values".[1]

Gandhi conceptualized an ideal social order on the basis of the given structural characteristics of the Indian economy and his fundamental philosophy of life. This social order was to be one of a nonviolent, non-exploitative, humanistic, and egalitarian society. Gandhi's doctrines of growth and employment relate to this particular kind of a social order. These doctrines suggest a process which, he believed, would bring about a transformation of the Indian socio-economic system, making it move towards its convergence with the ideal system that he envisioned.

The primary purpose here is to attempt a systematic exposition of these doctrines as a set of ideas and an exposure to an alternative system of thought, compared to conventional macroeconomics.

In our view, there are two major doctrines which may be called the Gandhian doctrines in this respect. One of them may be termed as the doctrine of growth and the other as the doctrine of employment.

The Doctrine of Growth

The Gandhian doctrine of economic growth is derived from a general theory of growth where growth is a function of a multitude of variables-economics, political, mental and moral. This general theory, therefore, relates to man as a whole-not just to the economic man or political man or the spiritual man. As such, it has to be responsive to the entire hierarchy of man's needs- economic, political, mental, and the moral. "The end to be sought", he wrote, "is human happiness combined with full mental and moral growth".[2]

The Gandhian doctrine of economic growth, being a part of his general theory of growth cannot meaningfully be formulated purely in economic terms.

In looking at growth as a multi-process activity, Gandhi recognized the possibility of conflict among various growth objectives-for instance, the conflict between material growth and moral growth. Because of his deep roots in Indian philosophy having a general anti-materialistic bias, and because of his deep concern for poverty among the Indian masses, his pragmatic mind pointed in the direction of reconciliation of conflicts among growth objectives. He was convinced that given proper planning and guidance, such conflicts would not necessarily emerge. He realized that without economic progress, poverty cannot be eradicated. At the same time, he was fully aware of the negative externalities that may result from uncontrolled economic progress. In Gandhian economics the notion of negative externality has to be defined in a much broader framework than is generally done in conventional theory of social costs. Here it must encompass all the distortions in various relationships in which man in involved, such as the relationship between the village and the city. Gandhi was convinced that with appropriate strategies for development and social experimentation, it would be possible to achieve a certain pattern and a certain process of economic growth that would not only minimize these potential distortions but would also immensely enhance the value of economic progress for man and society.

For a synthesis of various ideas that Gandhi expanded, one may construct what may be called a Gandhian Doctrine of Balanced Growth. In such a doctrine, one may identify the following elements:

(a) *Philosophical Balance:* a balance between economic progress and moral progress. To achieve such a balance, one must shift the emphasis from maximization to optimization of production, from abundance to adequacy of the production of material goods and service.

(b) Structural Balance: a balance between the rural and urban sectors of the economy. To achieve such a balance, growth of the urban sector much not take place at the expense of the rural sector. Here one must shift the emphasis from centralization to decentralization of economic activities.

(c) *Ecological Balance:* a balance in the relationship between man and his environment. Long before social concern grew over the environmental crisis in the Western industrial societies. Gandhi showed his awareness of this crisis as a natural by-product of uncontrolled economic progress and autonomous development of modern, large-scale technology. He stressed the need for deliberate choice of technology and for restraints on the level of production in order to maintain a proper balance between man and his environment.

(d) *Technological Balance:* a balance between small-scale and large-sale technologies, Gandhi's views on technology have often been misinterpreted. Gandhi was not opposed to the use of the modern technology as such. He was opposed to indiscriminate, non-selective adoption of imported technology, purely based on its effect on productive capacity. In the context of the Indian economy, he saw a tremendous need for the development of small-scale technology that would increase the efficiency of rural production without creating any technological displacement of labour. At the same time, he saw the need for large-scale technology for which the ideal location would be large urban centres. The point that he strongly emphasized is that the adoption of Western technology to economize on labour and expand production at the cost of rural de-industrialization and mass unemployment was not the proper choice of technology under the prevailing economic conditions in India. He endorsed a proper mix of technology in order to optimize the social benefits of science and technology?

(e) *Distributional Balance:* a balance in income distribution. Given the existence of gross inequality, to achieve a greater balance would require strategies to redistribute income. In the context of a growing economy, Gandhi's doctrine may be interpreted as a doctrine of dynamic equilibrium in the pattern of income distribution so that exploitation is reduced to the minimum. In modern growth theories, the problem of income distribution is generally assumed away. Gandhi was fully aware that a high rate of growth does not necessarily guarantee an equitable distribution of income. The later issue is tied up not so much with the rate of growth as with the pattern of growth. This is the reason why Gandhi was opposed to Western-style economic progress through urban-oriented large-scale industrialization. He would settle for a slower rate of growth for the sake of a greater diffusion of technology and productive capacity to revitalize the rural economy and also for the sake of a greater regional balance in the distribution of income.

A growth model that incorporates the elements described above may aptly be described as "magnificent dynamics" in a Gandhian way. This dynamics is for the "enlightened" man and not for just the "economic" man-man who wants to produce not only economic goods and services but also non-economic values that he needs for his total substance. Satisfying behaviour rather than maximizing behaviour would characterize man in a growing society that Gandhi envisioned.

This model has the characteristic of a dynamic equilibrium far beyond the scope of the economics of steady growth. It forcefully draws attention to the fact that if steady growth means growth without disturbance, all forms of disturbance must be recognized. A growing society in which balance is maintained between economic progress and moral progress, between the rural and the urban, between man and his environment, between small-scale and large-scale technology, in and income distribution, reflects the essence of the Gandhian version of dynamic equilibrium. It relevance to some of the most critical problems of modern society is self-evident.

The Doctrine of Employment

The Gandhian doctrine of employment is closely linked to his doctrine of growth. Gandhi has a profound concern for the problem of unemployment and poverty, especially in the rural sector of the Indian economy. He favoured such as pattern of economic growth and industrialization and such a choice of technology that would help alleviate rural unemployment and narrow the gap between the rural income levels and the urban income levels. In conventional economics of growth, it is not often recognized that a process of growth that maximizes production does not necessarily maximize employment. Much depends on the nature of the techno-structure of production. Gandhi was convinced that indeterminate adoption of Western technology of mass production would, in all likelihood, aggravate the problem of rural unemployment by destroying rural industries, even though national output would show significant expansion. His attack on the problem of rural unemployment was through decentralization of economic activities, revival and modernization of small-scale rural industries, and adaptation of modern technology to serve the needs of such industries. Gandhi's emphasis on rural industrialization and job creation in the rural sector is understandable in the context of the demographic rural-urban distribution in India. There the bulk of population is concentrated in the rural areas and the problems of unemployment and poverty are essentially of rural origin. Given the nature of such structural employment, in contrast with unemployment associated with deficiency of aggregate demand in industrial societies, the Gandhian doctrine of employment makes a great deal of sense. For a problem that is structural in nature, an appropriate remedy has to be some sort of restructuring of the economy. That is precisely what the Gandhian doctrine of employment is about.

If we look at the structure of the Indian economy in a simplified way, it can be broken down into two primary sectors: the rural sector and the urban sector. Gandhi was convinced that the hard core of the problems of unemployment and under-employment lies in the rural sector and although, strictly speaking, the problems were not peculiar only to the rural sector on the basis of sheer number, the rural problem does the greatest challenge to India's progress. He saw no alternative to the solution of this problem except through decentralization of economic activities and creation of viable rural economics. These economies were to be re-built with an optimum mix of industrial and agricultural enterprises, responsive to the needs to the villages and their immediate neighbours. It is not difficult to see how the Gandhian doctrine of Swadeshi relates to his doctrine of rural development and employment. If "Swadeshi" is defined as "the spirit in us which restricts us to the use and service of our immediate surroundings to the exclusion of the more remote",[4] it is obvious that rural industries and rural employment in the process of expansion, have to produce goods and service to meet the needs of not only the rural community but also those of he neighbouring communities. The implicit notion of service and the welfare content of employment importantly differentiates the Gandhian doctrine of employment from the conventional theory of employment in modern economics.

We have so far presented the Gandhian doctrine of employment in a macroeconomic context. At the micro-economic level also, the Gandhian doctrine introduces certain concepts that are distinctive. To him, work or employment is not only an economic concept but also a moral and meta-physical concept. It is a source of income without exploitation. It is an instrument of service. It is an instrument of self-realization. The moral and metaphysical notion ofwork, which Gandhi derived essentially from the Bhagavadgita, is noted for its famous doctrine of work.[5] This attitude towards work explains, to a great extent, why Gandhi put so much emphasis on the creation of more jobs rather than on the production of a larger output, if, at all, a choice has to be made.

The Gandhian doctrines of growth and employment, being consistent with his fundamental social philosophy, rightly belong to the Gandhian welfare economics. This particular formulation of the doctrines was dictated by his overriding concern for social and individual welfare. As is well known, welfare, to Gandhi, was a composite concept, partly economic, partly moral, and partly spiritual. One can almost conceptualize a sort of a grand social utility function-multidimensional social utility function in contrast to what is termed as the one-dimensional social utility function inconventional microeconomics. This approach forces the economicist to look beyond the purely economic needs of man. There are other worlds and other needs which it might be worthwhile for the economist to relate in a meaningful way. One may not necessarily accept the Gandhian view of other worlds and other needs. But the important issue in any case is: Should he recognize the other dimensions of life to which economics must relate? Gandhian economics strongly suggests that we should.

References

1. N.K. Bose, selections from Gandhi, Navajivan publishing House, Ahmedabad, 1948, p. 41.
2. M.K. Gandhi, All Men are Brothers, columbia University Press, New York, 1958, p. 124.
3. Amlan Datta, Aspects of Gandhian Economics, St. Martin's press, New York, 1970.
4. D.G. Tendulkar, Mahatma: Life of Mohandas Karamchand Gandhi, Publications Divispn, Ministry of Informatioin and Broadcasting, Govt, of India, New Delhi, 1960, Vol.I, p. 226.
5. B.N. Ganguli, Gandhi's Social Philosophy, Vikas Publishing House, New Delhi, 1973, p. 259.

4

Gandhi's Concept of Trusteeship : An Analysis

The purpose of this chapter to analyse Gandhi's concept of trusteeship in a fruitful and creative manner. The theory of trusteeship has been the subject of scholary evaluation by many writers who have thrown new light and significance on this particular concept. Gandhi's economic ideas have to be given serious consideration for solving the pressing socio-economic problems in an underdeveloped country like India. It is very rightly said that "Gandhiji is still a living challenge to the economic thinking, planning and action not only in his own country but in all the countries of the world".[1]

Whole of the world has reached the point of crisis today. Poverty, mass unemployment, inflation, environmental pollution and the insecurity of underdeveloped countries are prevailing. Not only the underdeveloped countries but the capitalistic advanced countries have also not been able to eradicate the poverty. In 1968 about 24 million people were below the poverty line in U.S.A., which includes more than a half of the black population. The environment pollution has posed a threat to the health and sanitary conditions and has increased the social cost of production. People are running out of patience and are looking for a system that alternative for both socialism and the capitalism.

Socialism assumes man to be a social unit who has no individuality of his own. All the men have been reduced to sub-human levels. They, of course, are assured of bread, though, at the cost of their freedom. There is nothing like private property. Everything belongs to the state. The welfare of a human soul is overlooked to serve the cause of soul-less state. The concentration of political and economic power in the hands of the state has made socialism synonym to state-capitalism. Human-rights are deemed to be "dispensable luxuries".

Capitalism, on the other hand, recognizes the individuality of man and assures the protection of his rights. All the human relationships are voluntary. But it has proved to be unable to provide bread to all. Freedom means nothing to a hungryman. Capitalism has resulted in great economic inequality and the exploitation of the have-nots by the haves. It has failed to narrow the gap between riches and the poors.

The third world has failed miserably in it bid for rapid industrialization, lured by the glamour of the west. They have overlooked their limitations and have walked into traps baited by the big owners. The developed countries have made the under developed countries dependent on them for "aids" and "technology". The big powers can, thus exert a great influence on their policy matters. The quest for industrialisation in underdeveloped countries has benefitted a few privileged ones and the multinationals. While the majority of people are striving hard for survival.

The experiment with the democratic- socialistic system, as in India, has proved to be disasterous. The idea behind this was to benefit from the merits of both the capitalism and socialism. But what we have got is the evils of both the system. Bureaucracy, Red-tapism, Unnecessary controls by the state, mass-poverty great economic inequalities and unbalanced growth are a few to cite.

So what is needed is a system that provides both bread and freedom to the man who is both an individual and freedom to the man who is both an individual and social man. This system should be free of the evils of capitalism or socialism. And the concept of "Trusteeship" only can provide such a system. It only can show the way out of the state of fix the world is in.

Trusteeship means that the possessor of wealth should consider himself as a trustee and use the wealth for the good of others.

The concept of trusteeship was derived by Mahatma Gandhi

from his study of jurisprudence snell's principles of Equality and the Gītā. Trusteeship means all money and property originally belongs to society and those who are possessing it are only the trustees of the society whose duty is to increase the earning and value of the trust property. He should charge only that much from the trust property as is absolutely essential for his subsistence and honorable living. Excess of one's income over and above one's is a social surplus to be employed for the benefit of the society. Breach of trust is a crime and is punishable underlaw.[2] Under the trusteeship theory of Gandhi certain limited property rights are admissible. The Trusteeship theory of Gandhi does not recognise the inherent, unrestricted, irresponsible and absolute right of private property.

He held the view that property was a concept that arose only within the confines of human society and as such it belonged to the society at large as much as to particular individuals and hence it must be used for the welfare of one and all. In such a consideration the mental or physical talent or wealth of individuals have to be looked upon as a trust and consequently have to be used for the benefit of the society. Gandhi's trusteeship did not recognise hereditary inheritance of property. He visualised a transition or transformation from individual ownership a community or trust ownership in the longrun. The profit motive was conspicuous by its absence in trusteeship. Trustees may be get remuneration for the work done through common consent of workers and the state. There must be parity between the remuneration of the trustees and the workers and should normally not be more than the latter. The managerial skills of the trustees, the talent and expertise of labour was neither to be exploited nor used to subserve vested interests of the few. On the contrary, society as a whole must derive the benefits. Such a theory of trusteeship was not contrary to the interests of the capitalists but it sought common good through a proper utilization of their experience and talent. For Gandhi, trusteeship involved the building of consensus of a society for implementing it for social good, Gandhi wanted that the rich should become the trustees of the society by sharing their surplus wealth with the poor and under privileged. This argument was advanced by him in the belief that society in general was an extension of the particularistic family.

Gandhi gave the concept of Trusteeship "the sanction of philosophy and religion behind it".[3] He was deeply influenced by

Ruskin's *Unto This Last* and he was of the firm opinion that by nature all human beings were equal and there should not be any economic discrimination or disparity among different individuals in respect of income, consumption and other bare necessities of life. The deep and widening message of Gita and the Bible made him believe in man's capacity for goodness, altruism of human nature, and moral consciousness of man, transformation of heart etc. Non-violence in thought and demeanour was the main spirit of his theory of trusteeship which could be used as a weapon against those who were unwilling to divert their personal property into public wealth. As a hard-headed realist, Gandhi in his own life time was aware of the deep influence of human craving for material comforts of life which caused a few to accumulate wealth of the society, disproportioned to their needs and at the cost of the majority who were ignorant, poor and living a life of ceaseless misery. Against this background Gandhi formulated his theory of trusteeship which could bring about equal distribution of the accumulated wealth for societal happiness through emphasis on metaphysical and religious aspects of life.

Trusteeship implies a voluntary acceptance by the rich to use their possessions for the needs of the society. Elimination of exploitation and inequality are the goals of trusteeship. That is why it is a policy for distributive justice.

The idea of *Trusteeship* has been inspired by Gandhiji from the concept of '*Non-Possession*' of capita. Private property is not denied. The intervention of state in economic matter is least desirable except in case of public utilities and heavy industries that are necessary for the strength of the country. So the capitalists or the property owners are not eliminated from the scene. They are asked to act as trustees of the property they are managing, for the people. They are here given an opportunity to convert themselves from "*Self-interests*" to the cause of humanity. Though they are still managing the property or the business, but they no more possess it. Their entrepreneurial talents and their wealth are the part and parcel of society. They are holding their wealth in trust for people of the society. They are not permitted to possess more than what is required for their own requirements. After reducing this part from the surplus earned is either to be surrendered to the society or to be re-invested. If the property owners failed to cooperate, their properties can be confiscated by legislation with the minimum use of violence.

The decentralisation of industries and absence of conspicuous consumption are necessary for the success of trusteeship model. Here the services of state are asked for. The development of infrastructure and transportation will help in decentralization. Transportation costs should be insignificant in deciding over the location of an industry. This will help in rural industrialization and will help in the development of rural area.

As no one is to consume more than one needs, there will be redistribution of income, for the better, from the rich to the poor. There will be automatic reductions in economic inequalities and poverty will have to leave the scene. Decentralization of industries along with trusteeship shall work for the independence of villages, and if the villages and cities are self-sufficient the nation will automatically be. We can obviate our dependence in foreign aid to bridge the gap between the capital required and the capital available. The country shall be self-sufficient in all respects.

One more feature of Trusteeship is that it will dispense with the use of middlemen. If the villages are self-sufficient, the producers will be in direct contact with their customers. The absence of monetary incentives will also discourage hoarding and speculation. This will limit the use of money to a minimum and will give the stability to prices. Supply can always be adjusted accordingly to demand as there is perfect mobility.

The allocation of resources will be most efficient under trusteeship, as trusteeship no scope for monopolies or monopolistic competition. As there is perfect mobility of factors of production between different regions, there are homogeneous products (Labelling or advertising are dispensed with), there is perfect knowledge of markets, free entries and "free exists of inefficients" are there, perfect competition can be realised in the system, which makes the most efficient use of resources. This also makes maximum social welfare attainable.

Gandhi mentioned equal distribution of wealth as one of the thirteen items in his constructive programme. In short, the real implication of equal distribution is that each man must have the where withal to supply his essential and natural needs. So the real meaning of economic equality is to each according to his needs. Gandhi did not want to produce a dead equality where every person becomes or is rendered incapable of using his ability to the utmost possible extent for such a society carries with it seeds of ultimate destruction. This leads us to the crucial problem of economic through advocated by Gandhi viz., the doctrine of Trusteeship.

Gandhi wanted the richmen to held their wealth in trust for the poor or give it up for them. He wanted that the rich should become trustees of their surplus wealth for the good of society. Thus the society was to be regarded only as an extension of the family. We have to realize that if the wealth accumulates in the hands of any, it is not due to his own efforts alone. It is due to the collective effort alone. It is due to the collective effort of all and so it belongs to all in society. We have to understand that the individuals are only the means to produce wealth and each holds it for the benefit of all. The father rarely thinks that whatever he earns is entirely his and due to his sole effort. He works for the family-thus giving every member of the family the right to his undivided Hindu families. If man can care for the limited circle of his family he can surely realize that the entire wealth in his hands belongs to the society in general. He is only the guardian of the wealth and should use it for the good of all.

It may be asked whether such a change is possible in human nature. Such changes have certainly taken place in individuals. What is to be done, if the rich do not become trustees of their wealth inspite of the utmost effort? Gandhiji advocates non-violent, non-co-operation and civil disobedience as the right and in falliable remedy, for the rich cannot accumulate wealth without the co-operation of the poor in society.

It is a fundamental law that nature produce what is strictly needed for our wants from day to day. Hence, if everybody is self-sufficient and took just what is needed for himself and nothing more, no one would die of starvation in this world. Any one who appropriate more than the minimum that is necessary for him is guilty of theft. This is a grand ideal. But in actual practice, is it possible to follow? Can such an ideal be realized?

The doctrine is born out of common sense and sure belief of what is practical. Change of heart is all that is needed on the part of individuals. To those who are already wealthy or would not she their desire for wealth. Gandhi's advice is that they should use their wealth for service. True, Gandhi's first enunciated the theory vis-a-vis the socialists who wanted to deprive the zamindars and ruly chiefs of all their privileges and wealth.

With the passage of time, Gandhi added economic and sociological content to the rather moralistic conception of trusteeship. The basic assumptions of the doctrine are:

I. Trusteeship provides a means of transforming the present capitalist order of society into an egalitarian one.

II. It does not recognize any right of private ownership of property except in as much as it may be permitted by society.

III. It does not exclude legislative regulation of the ownership and use of wealth.

IV. Thus, under state-regulated trusteeship an individual will not be free to hold or use his wealth for selfish satisfaction or in disregard of the interests of society.

V. Just as it is a proposed to fix a decent minimum living wage, even so a limit should be fixed for the maximum income that could be allowed to any person in society. The difference between such minimum and maximum incomes should be reasonable and equitable and variable from time to time so much so that the tendency would be towards obliteration of the difference.

VI. Under the Gandhian economic order, the character of production will be determined by social necessity and not by personal whim or greed.[4]

The formula is realistic and also flexible. The question, "How many can be real trustees?" is beside the point. Gandhi felt that if the rich do not become trustees voluntarily, force of circumstance will compel them to do so unless have no desire for averting the disaster. Trusteeship is an attempt to secure the best use of property for the people by competent hands. Gandhi's basic belief was that everything belonged to God and was from God. Therefore, it was for His people as a whole not for particular individual. When the individual had more than his proportionate portion he became a trustee of that portion for God's people........ If this truth was imbibed by the people generally, it would become legalized and trusteeship would become a legalized institution. Gandhi hoped that the ideal of Trusteeship would become a gift from India to the people of the world. It should be noted that Trusteeship is the first step towards the realization of decentralized economic order. Decentralization is the technique of non-violent democracy.

Gandhi always stressed simplicity and satisfaction of the basic needs of human life as the cornerstone of his entire economic philosophy. He was of the opinion that the earth was endowed with enough resources to meet every man's basic needs.[5] But the greed of men for competitive acquisitiveness leading to concentration of wealth in the hands of a small previleged and influential section of the society positively deprived the basic needs of the majority in the society. Through trusteeship, Gandhi wanted to establish an equitable economic order through a proper scheme of distribution of the accumulated wealth to all members of the society. But more important than this consideration was his concern to remove selfishness from human beings by appealing to the moral consciousness of the individuals. Gandhi held the view that since the state was a soulless machine and represented violence in a concentrated and organised form.[6] The state was unable to appeal to the superior moral ethos of men with a view to transform their minds and hearts from selfishness and acquisitiveness to one of common good. In Gandhi, the institution of trusteeship was created to primarily provide an opportunity to capitalists and land lords in whose hands a huge quantum of wealth of the society accumulated, to voluntarily transfer their wealth to the society. The capitalistic were expected to act as trustees along with other representatives of the society. This was prescribed to avoid the confiscation of surplus wealth through coercion by state action or by the techniques of class struggle. Though Gandhi was not a socialist by conviction, yet his prognosis of the Indian situation led him to believe that a dichotomy in the interests of the privileged and under privileged or rich and poor could have disastrous consequences for India. Trusteeship was indeed a non-violent alternative to class war for and mass violence, since it emphasizes the ethico-religious dimensions in human beings.

The unbridgeable gulf between the peasants and the Landlords, the workers and mill-owners, the people of the states and Indian princes, the classes and the masses deeply exercised Gandhi's mind. In his scheme of things there is nothing inherently conflictual or contradictory in the interests of the capitalists, and Labourers. Unlike the Marxists, Gandhi believed that the labourers and the capitalists could work together in harmony like a great family, with each functioning for mutual good and mutual advancement.[7] Gandhi therefore held that the capitalists were to regard themselves as trustees "for those on whom he depends for the making the retention and increase in his capital".[8] The objective of the trusteeship theory was to destroy capitalism and not the capitalists.[9]

The concept of trusteeship economy which Gandhi built up systematically was a pioneering effort on his part. His emphasis was on idealism and innate goodness of human beings in society, the social concern, the fierce determination and unshakable dedication which could bring about a socio-economic order some what superior to the acquistiveness of the private enterprise and the all-powerful democratic socialism in which the individual was scarified at the altar of the state. Hence, trusteeship can be regarded as "an economic thought in itself that differs significantly from both capitalism and socialism in many respects."[10] It was a non-violent alternative to legal expropriation and class war against mixed economy.

In effect, Gandhi was putting forth the viewpoint that every individual must do physical labour to satisfy his most essential needs[11] and at the same time none had the right to accumulate property or wealth more than what he needed at any given point of time.[12] These two basic principles of Gandhian economy order could usher in complete equality between capitalists and the labourer, the rich and the poor. Gandhi was not prepared to recognize any in equality in human beings except physical inequalities and to him they could be understood in their proper perspective. He rightly held the view that there was no justification for "the glaring difference between the classes and the masses, the prince and the pauper, by saying that the former need more. That will be idle sophistry and travesty of my argument".[13] In a society where mass illiteracy was of a high order and the hold of superstition dogma and tradition very pervasive, existing inequalities were the result of the people's ignorance of their moral and legal rights. Socio-economic and political inequalities could disappear with the realisation of the people's natural strength.[14] In the circumstances, voluntary renunciation or riches and power was the only alternative, failing which a violent and bloody revolution was inevitable with its concomitant of new reforms or radical transformation of society.[15] Gandhi felt that trusteeship was a potent weapon to remove the ills of a capitalist society by transforming it into an egalitarian society based on justice and fair play. He had equally firm faith in the ultimate goodness of human good. He recognised private property as an unnecessary evil at worst and in so far as it served the interest of the society at its best. If voluntary surrender of excess wealth or property was not forth coming, Gandhi was prepared to recommend coercion for abolition of ownership. This was to be done so that individual property was not used to serve sectional interests of the society. Under state regulated trusteeship, the difference between the minimum and maximum wages would be reasonable and equitable so that a rational and functional social order could emerge, on the basis of equality. In the Gandhian economic order, social necessity and social good rather than individual selfishness and idiosyncrasy would determine the nature and substance of production of goods in society.[16]

Even in international economic relations, we have to keep in mind the challenge of world poverty and the chronic disparity. A recent study by UNCTAD has revealed that the multinational giants not only stifle the economy (through choking of normal trade channels, direct brand competition, price cutting and price manipulation, buying over the competition and vilification of rival brands) but also undermine the very sovereignty of many countries. They think in terms of profits. Discrimination in matters of appointment remuneration, and promotion is practised neglecting the rightful claims of indigenous personnel. They corrupt officials and politicians of the host countries.[17] According to Gunnar Myrdal, the "classical assumption that international trade initiates a tendency towards gradual equalisation of income as among different countries stands out as obviously unrealistic and against all experience.[18] Equality of treatment is equitable only among equals. Hence, it is very necessary that the multinational corporations should become truly multinational and should at as trustees of economic growth and development throughout the world. If it fails, it will lead to an endless world-conflict. It is not under development and poverty that constitute the threat to peace, for the people of the world are long used to. It is continued existence and aggravations of inequalities in development-the rich/richer, poor/poorer nationals dichotomy which is daily growing ever wider and so glaring that they become inequitous which is the foreteller of the final conflagration.[19]

Political commentators have carefully examined the economic concept of trusteeship and have severely critised it on the ground that it was a view point of considerable antiquity. It has also been suggested that the trusteeship theory has hindered the socio-economic transformation of traditional society into that of a modern industrial order. Gandhi sought an ethical solution to an economic problem. He under estimated the powerful play of psychological factors like human greed and acquisitiveness in the material world. Gandhi seems to apply an ethical frame work towards the building up of an equitable economic order based on trusteeship. He took a very simplistic view of group dynamics and group conflicts in a feudal or traditional world order. In essence, the theory and practice of trusteeship was neither clearly developed into a philosophical system nor a functionally relevant theory that was capable of being put into practice. Gandhi's emphasis on satisfying basic needs of human beings and the simplicity of life were contrary to the prevailing social environment which laid very heavy emphasis on a material civilization. It must be recognized that "simplicity is also a relative term: it depends upon the circumstances and on the surroundings, and in the modern world, where science has made great striking progress and industrialistion has taken grip over the whole human society, now to say that we will run away from it would be not only unreal, but it would be giving up good things in order to escape from bad things".[20] Under such circumstances acceptance of trusteeship principle would turn out to be a reversion to industrial primitivism in an age characterised by the scientific and technological revolution.

Gandhi in his lifetime persuaded the capitalist class to act as trustees of the people. It has been said that "Gandhiji was rather disillusioned in the end and held that his capitalist friends could never become the trustees of the people. The capitalist went to him for their own purpose mostly...... but Gandhiji could not turn the heart of even one capitalist. They remained what they were ...".[21]

Gandhi was not clear in his understanding of the nature and impact of the capitalist system, which was mostly a hindrance to rapid economic growth. His naive belief that capitalism with its fundamental emphasis on generation of surplus or profit would transform itself in such a manner that working class would be put on an equal footing with the capitalist class. In a traditional society like India, the wealthy class was not in favour of sharing their wealth with others in society on a voluntary basis. This was because of the fact in a traditional society accumulation of wealth was equivalent to power, influence and prestige in the society. No capitalist was prepare to lose his dominant position by voluntary acceptance of trusteeship. To argue, as Gandhi did, that he was not against capitalists as such but against capitalism as a creed, is a contradiction in terms. In the capitalist system the capitalists constituted an integral element of the system. If the capitalist system is abolished the capitalists would also be exterminated along with the system. In its place the socialist order could merge with full state control over the means of production. Therefore, to argue that capitalism could be destroyed without eliminating the capitalists is meaningless and irrational. It can be surmised that Gandhi was trying to build up a via media alternative between capitalism and socialism but unfortunately his attempt proved to a magnificent failure.

Broadly it can be said that Gandhi's ideas on trusteeship were right theoretically but the world will not implement his ideas for the simple reason that it is too late to change the path it has bestowed upon itself. When the world has reached a high state of industrialization, how can it put the cloth back and embrace industrial primitivism? Moreover, there are many inconsistencies and gaps in his theory of trusteeship, and it would require a great deal of expertise and thought on the part of contemporary scholars to develop a viable and relevant theory of trusteeship applicable to the modern period.

Further, Gandhi was also wrong in some of his fundamental principles, when he sought to impose an ethical criterion to work out mechanics for his theory of trusteeship. To consider every problem from the moral perspective irrespective of the three dimensions of past, present and the future made his theory of trusteeship static and artificial. It is indeed very surprising to realise that Gandhi lacked an insight into the complex historical process. Had it not been for his blindness to history, he would not have applied a spiritual frame work to an essentially material problem, with which his theory of trusteeship was primarily trying to find solutions. His understanding of the relationship between material well being and spiritual pursuit was faulty and simplistic.

Gandhi emphasised simplicity and an ascetic life as the basis of his personal life and he transferred these values into the wider sphere of the society. It does not require much justification to argue that he over-generalised a personal experience on which his theory of trusteeship rested and certainly this was a weak and shaky foundation.

Gandhi believed that non-violent, non cooperation could transform the social structure in the desired manner. The theory of trusteeship was an intrinsic part of his overall scheme of peaceful transformation of the society. But this is not supported by the situation prevailing in the contemporary world. It can be said with considerable force that war, conquest and violence are basic to human nature, and even in Gandhi's own life time this was true. This being the case, how can a non-violent egalitarian socio-economic order be built up?

On the whole, one can say that Gandhi's concept of trusteeship may appear to be irrelevant to the modern age, but in a country like India which has a traditional social order with its attendant emphasis on religious and metaphysical aspects of life, Gandhian economic thought could be of use to solve the ongoing problem of mass poverty. The trusteeship theory "cannot become reality without a thorough social awakening. Only then the owning class will recognise the reality and be trustees either voluntarily or in the wake of the non-cooperation".[22] It must be said that absolute trusteeship is unattainable since it was abstract and Utopian in its thrust and significance.

Before we close, it is necessary to discuss whether Trusteeship is practicable. Gandhi had launched its experiment in common wealth pattern of ownership, enjoyment and management in 1904. The next on a vaster scale was tried in his Tolstoy Farm of 1000 acres. Critics say that Gandhi could change the heart of only one person a half-himself and to some extent of Jamnalal Bajaj. Gandhi himself said:- "Only Jamnalalji came near, but only near it.[23] However Gandhiji's campaign against the British rule was, an instance of implementation of trusteeship in the political field. Gandhi through satyagraha and other methods prevailed upon the British Government to fulfil the pledge of trusteeship and divest itself of all political privileges. His non-violent struggle to make Britain fulfil her responsibilities as a trustee was crowned with success.[24] He had also advised the former Indian Princes to act and behave as trustees of their subjects. During the opening ceremony of Benaras Hindu University on 4th Feb, 1916, Gandhiji said "There is no salvation for India unless you strip yourselves of the jewellery and hold it in trust for your countrymen in India".[25] He was frank enough when he said.... in the independent India, the whole of it (Property) belonged to the people. Nothing of it belonged to the princes as individuals. Their claim could only be sustained by their being trustees of the people"[26] So after the lapse of paramountcy, two-thirds of country's area under princely states with the exception of one or two, gracefully handed over their powers and properties to the rightful owners the people.[27] In social field Gandhiji approved of the enactment of the legislation to compel the trustees of Hindu temples who claimed a privilege in refusing entry to Harijans into the temples. After Gandhi's death, Vinobaji through his country wide Bhoodan-Gramdan movements demonstrated the concrete manifestation of the same principles in action. In Bhoodan movement, nearly 46 lakhs acres of land was collected through voluntary gift. In Gramdan movement, the ownership of land was vested in the village community.

In recent times, the noted cricketer and industrialists Sri. Vijay Merchant made on experiment of the trusteeship idea in his textile concern". The Hindustan shipping and Weaving Mills" in Bombay. He has found excellent labour-management relations. Under the Zero Defect Programme, the defects in productivity has been reduced resulting in higher production.

The "trust" has of late begun to play a part in the evolution of the 19th Century capitalism into social responsibility.[26] This is reflected in the remarkable growth in recent years of common ownership enterprises in the U.K. and elsewhere. The British Parliament has also passed industrial common ownership Act, 1976. In U.K. Scott-Bedar common wealth founded in 1920 converted itself into common ownership, common wealth in 1951. In 1975, it won queen's Award for Industry. On every count, the level of wages and salami productivity, sanitation and health, it was found superior to any of its competition capitalist enterprises. Another example of common ownership are John Lewis partnership with 25000 employees, Sunderlandia Limited, the Rowen Community etc. In U.S.A. to cite an outstanding example, seers Rocbuck a great company has been steadily transferring profits for the past 50 years with the results that the company's contributions to the employees share fund rose to about 120 billion a few years ago, shared by 310,000 employees. It West Germany the ideas of regulating the relationship between two parties in industry on a basis of trust was introduced in 1895 by Prof. Ernst Abbe in Carl Zeiss works at Jenn has been working well. The concept of Industrial Democracy and Autonomy has flourished in Scandinavian countries particularly in Sweden, where the manual workers and the salaries employees reached a historical agreement to set up workers councils to solve their problems between themselves and with regard to the basic interests of the nation and the consumers. Such Joint councils have been set up in all firms having 25 or more employees. In Japan, paternalistic type of industrial relations have developed when a worker gets married, the company pays his full wedding bill. The Mexico, the constitution has established a permanent national commission of workers, employers and Government to determine the distribution of profits. The commission is encouraging participation of workers in day-to-day management.

The Gandhian theory of Trusteeship has a permanent truth and its validity is being more and more realised the West today. A. E. Morgan writes, "Modern life with its rapidly growing complexities greatly increases the number of situations in which the only sound relation is that of trustee and the growth of a sense of responsibility has not been sufficiently rapid to meet these changing conditions".[28] In the field of industrial ownership and management too, some thinkers and practical men of affairs in the democratic West are coming to the conclusion that a superior alternative to both the capitalist and state ownership and management is a new form of ownership and management based on what might be termed the 'Principle of Trusteeship'.

As compared with the situation herein India, we could say that considerable work has been done in Europe. The practical steps taken by businessmen in Europe who voluntarily turned as trustees in the Gandhian sense and the systematic studies such as *The New Form of Ownership and The Responsible company* have performed a vital and essential service. They have lifted up trusteeship economy from mere good intentions and ethical formulations and given it concrete, practical and judicial shape. It is felt here in India whether state regulated trusteeship would solve the problem.

Gandhiji says that "Absolute Trusteeship is an abstraction like Euclid's definition of a point and is equally unattainable. But if were strive for it, we shall be able to go further in realizing a state of equality on earth than by any other method".[29] He further said: "If only we could make people conscious of this power-the power of non-violent, non-Co-operation, the realization of the ideal of trusteeship would follow as surely as morning follows night".[30]

Is the trusteeship concept relevant for the present day society?

Yes. Trusteeship stands for distributive justice, economic equality and radical change of structure, all of which are pressing needs of society to day.

References

1. Shriman Narayan, Towards Gandhian plan, (New Delhi, S. Chand and Co. Ltd., 1978), p. 92.
2. M.K. Gandhi : Young India, April 24, 1937.
3. Harijan, 16-2-1939, p. 376.
4. M.K. Gandhi, Harijan, October 25, 1952.
5. G. Parthasarathy, "Integrated Rural Development:- Concept, Theoretical Base, and contradictions", ed. T. Mathew, Rural Development in India (New Delhi, Agricole publishing Academy, 1981) p. 31.
6. The Modern Review, October, 1935, p. 413.
7. S. Naqvi, "Economic Thinking of Gandhi - The Theory of Trusteeship". ed. S.C. Biswas, Gandhi Theory and practice Social impact and Contemporary Relevance. (Simla, Indian Institute of Advanced Studies, 1969), p. 212.
8. Young India, March 26, 1931, p. 49.
9. Ibid; March 26, 1931, p. 49.
10. M.M. Sury, "Relevance of Gandhian Economic Thought for social transformation", Political and Economic Review, 7th Oct. 1970, p.5.
11. The Harijan, September, 29, 1935.

12. The Harijan, August, 25, 1940.
13. The Harijan, March 31, 1946, p. 63.
14. The Harijan, Sept., 2, 1942, p. 249.
15. The Harijan, June 1, 1947, p. 172.
16. Pyarelal, Mahatama Gandhi - Last phase (Ahmedabad, Navjivan, 1938), p.634.
17. Suzuki, M. " Rising Tide of Resentment against Japanese Business in S.E. Asia", in the Economic Times, Bombay, 22, 1972.
18. The Calcutta of World poverty, p. 274.
19. Adiseshiah, M.S. Dy. Dir. General, UNESCO, quoted, R.B. Upadhayaya, Ibid, P. 317.
20. Morarji Desai, "Gandhi and the contemporary world", in K.P. Misra, S.C. Gangal, (ed) Gandhi and the contemporary world (Delhi, Chanakya Publications, 1981) pp. 14-15.
21. Acharya Kripalani, Gandhian outlook and Techniques, (New Delhi, Ministry of Education, Government of India, 1953), pp. 116-117.
22. B.K. Bhattacharya, "Trusteeship, means of Equalitarian Social change", Janata, 14 May, 1978.
23. Harijan, 12-4-42.
24. Gadre, kamla, Indian way to socialism, New Delhi, 1966, p. 46.
25. Natesan, G.N. "Speeches and writings of M. Gandhi, p. 322.
26. Tendulkar D.G., Mahtama, Vol. V, p. 221.
27. Goyder, George, C.C. Desai Memorial Lecture on "Some Thoughts Trusteeship as a principle of administration and Govt. News letter of the Trusteeship foundation, Bombay No. 6.
28. A.E. Morgan, The Long Road, p. 75.
29. M.K. Gandhi, Trusteeship, Series 13, p. 12.
30. Pyarelal, Towards, New Horizans, p. 93.

5
Gandhi's Concept of Decentralisation : An Analysis

"It is said that Taj Mahal looks different to different people, depending on where they are standing and particularly what time of the day it is. I feel rather like that about Bapu"[1] says an apostle of Gandhi. The authors also feel that Gandhi looks different to different writers, depending on what concept of Gandhi they are studying and particularly with what viewpoint they wish to project Gandhi's multi dimensional contribution. Various political scientists, economists, sociologists and spiritualists have studied Gandhi's political, economic, social religious and spiritual concepts. Some of these scholars are of the view that Gandhi's ideas are pragmatic and always relevant with some modifications, irrespective of the time and place. But to some others, Gandhi's ideas are entirely irrelevant and inapplicable in an age of scientific and technological progress with its attendant complexity of issues. Whatever may be the contrary views in this ongoing debate on Gandhism, one thing is beyond doubt that Ghandhism presents a new, dynamic, revolutionary and rational approach to existing political and Socio-economic problems. Shriman Narayanan says that "the more I think about diverse problems facing India at present, the more I feel convinced that Gandhian approach alone will be able to solve our difficulties on a lasting basis".[2]

Gandhiji, popularly known as Mahatma Gandhi, held a unique position in the public life of this country for about more than four decades as the leader of not only great political movement, but as a moral and social reformer with an immense and unprecedented following. Crores of men and women of different castes, creeds, classes and diverse occupations, in the West as well as in the East, rose to the occasion to the call of his practical idealism. He had really identified himself completely with the toiling and poverty stricken masses of India and he lived as the poorest of his countrymen lived. Gandhiji had, in fact, imbibed a rare insight into the various problems facing the country to which others could not.

Gandhiji was not well acquainted with the Economics in technical sense of the term. He cannot be placed in the list of Economists of the world of in the modern sense. However, his approach to the economic problems and their solution has been quite unique. In fact, his social and economic thoughts were largely shaped by his own practical experience, wide and searching travel, intensive readings of Gītā, Bible, Tolstoy, Ruskin and Marx etc. He had a strong feeling, and rightly too, that the economics, like politics cannot be divorced from morals. Thus, he viewed economics and economic problems in an entirely different way. However, his ideas on economic problems revealed a pragmatic and more rational approach specially for economic problems faced by our country.

We proceed with the assumption that in the contemporary period of change and conflict, political instability and inefficiency in administration, the absence of a viable economic policy and the failure to achieve five plan targets, the only alternative is to examine critically and dispassionately Gandhian economic and political ideas as a rational approach to our problems of national reconstruction and regeneration. Hence, it is our objective to make a comprehensive and systematic analysis of the Gandhian concept of decentralisation in its political and economic dimensions.

The concept of decentralisation has been much discussed and debated for a long time by economic thinkers, political scientists and social analysts. The concept of decentralisation is not of recent origin. Writers, social reformers, political philosophers like the anarchists, early socialist, Rousseau, modern pluralists and liberal socialists emphasized the concept of decentralisation of economic and political powers of the state.

An attempt has been made here to explain Gandhi's concept of political and economic decentralisation separately. But sometimes it has become inevitable to explain both simultaneously to sustain the flow of argument and to maintain academic objectivity and perspective in analysis.

Gandhi's concept of decentralisation does not stand in isolation but it is shaped by other concepts and ideas Gandhi's complex and dynamic personality was made up of an original mind that encompassed the whole range of issues and problems in human affairs. He preached non-violence, stressed on the moral aspects of life, he fought for freedom and equality of the poor; opposed state control over individuals, pleaded for swaraj, explained the concept of "*trusteeship*" for the welfare of all, opposed big industries to save cottage and village industries and preached Swadeshi and Khadi. All these concepts, directly or indirectly, flow from the theme of decentralisation. It is also our purpose to establish a clear cut linkage between these concepts and the theme of decentralisation.

Political Decentralisation

Gandhi preached non-violence as a means and as an end in itself. Non-violence is the basic tenet of political and economic decentralisation. To Gandhi non-violence was the kingdom of heaven and if we seek it first everything shall be added unto us.[3] He also said that for him "ahiṁsā comes before swaraj,...... Ahiṁsā must be placed before everything else while it is professed".[4] Ahiṁsā means not only refraining from killing any life out of anger or selfish purpose, but it means the avoidance of injury to anything it thought, word or deed.[5]

Gandhi was of the firm opinion that exploitation was the essence of violence as it harmed the personality of individuals. He believed that exploitation became a reality when power was concentrated in a single body like the state. The state represents, (says Gandhi) "Violence in a concentrated and organised form. The individual has a soul, but as the state is a soul less machine, it can never be weaned from violence to which it owes its very existence".[6]

The logical connection between decentralisation of political power and his concept of ahiṁsā become very clear. On the one hand, Gandhi was the foremost champion of Ahiṁsā and on the other hand he held the view that the state represented violence in an undiluted and organised form. Hence perseverance of ahiṁsā or non-violence was of the utmost importance. Violence must be avoided, and to eliminate violence concentration of power must be avoided, through decentralisation of power from the state. Gandhi looked "upon an increase in the power of the state with the greatest fear, because although while apparently doing good by minimising exploitation, it does the greatest harm to mankind destroying individuality, which lies at the root of all progress".[7] Destroying individuality means exploitation which led to violence. Therefore, to avoid violence and to ensure maximum flowering of the human personality, decentralisation of political power must become an end of a progressive and welfare oriented society. The question arises as to whether this kind of non-violence which Gandhi visualised could be secured in a reasonable manner in the modern state. Gandhi himself was not sure about it. He believed that "a Government cannot succeed in becoming entirely non-violent, because it represents all the people. I do not today conceive of such a golden age. But I do believe in the possibility of a predominantly non-violent society. And I am working for it".[8]

According to Gandhi, political power of the state was not an end in itself, but "one of the means enabling the people to better their condition in every department of life".[9] Gandhi saw human progress in human happiness by combining all mental and moral growth,[10] the greatest good of all rather that the greatest good of the greatest number. Gandhi was of the firm opinion that to what extent the ends were pure, to that extent the means would be pure. He always said that if the means was proper the ends would take care of themselves". Gandhi's objective is securing human happiness with full mental and moral in itself. Gandhi maintained that such an "end can be achieved under decentralisation. Centralization as a system is inconsistent with non-violent structure of Society".[12]

Gandhi sincerely believed that the state represented an organisation based on force. It manifested its coercive power through compulsion and exploitation of the individuals in the society. Gandhi held the view that any action of the state which was not voluntary in nature was immoral, since in his scheme of thinking every action was judged from the touch stone of ethical propriety. He argued that "no action which is not voluntary can be called moral... so long as we act like machines, there can be no question of morality. If we want to call an action moral, it should have been done consciously, and as a matter of duty".[13]

Political power was just a means, not an end in itself. It was a means to regulate national life through national representatives. Gandhi reasoned that national life could become perfect if it was self-regulated, where in no representation becomes necessary. There is then a state of enlightened anarchy. In such a state the sovereignty vests in everyone who is his ruler. He governs himself in a manner that he respects the freedom of his neighbor and in all such activity there is no political power because there is no state.[14]

Gandhi was an individualist par excellence and he argued in favour of a stateless society. His concept of "enlightened anarchy" will have to be viewed in such a context. Gandhi always felt that the state was an instrument of coercion which undermined the freedom of individuals. Such a position is a kin to the Marxist view of the state. The Gandhian and Marxist position that the state is an instrument of coercion is similar only in form, but in substance there methods of bringing about a stateless society are totally contradictory. Gandhi believed in the efficacy of non-violence for the socio-economic and spiritual salvation of the individual, while the Marxists stress upon a violent revolution which could eventually bring about the withering away of the state. Apparently, Gandhi and the Marxists are anarchists, but their similarity does not go far enough. Gandhi and the Marxist are individualists but with a fundamental difference, one exalting the individual is no uncertain terms while the other submerges the individual in an authoritarian state.

According to one ocholar Gandhi visualised the goal of enlightened anarchy in three phases. In the initial stage the goal was one of immediate swaraj based on nationalisation and in the second stage the objective was to bring about a non-violent state through the evolution of village republics. In the final stage the purpose was to achieve Ramraj. The non-violent state would be transformed into a pure democracy changed with the ideal of enlightened anarchy.[15]

Swaraj, a non-violent state and Ramraj are significant mile stones in Gandhi's concept of decentralisation in its comprehensive form. Village swaraj is another crucial element of his concept of decentralisation. The term swaraj owes its origin to ancient Hindu philosophy. Swaraj means self rule. Gandhi in a consistent and articulate fashion pleaded for village swaraj. It meant that every village must be an independent and self-contained unit in itself. He was convinced that "the small communities can certainly act as forces for the stabilisation of personality by creating a nucleus of organic socio-psychological density. An intense civic and social participation is possible".[16] Gandhi visualised villages to be self-sustained and autonomous, so that every village is capable of managing its affairs, itself, even to the extent of defending itself against the on slaught of the environment. Swaraj is a comprehensive term and infinitely greater than the concept of independence.[17] Gandhi was clear in his mind on this issue and he did not want his theme of village swaraj to be misunderstood by anybody. Self rule and self- sufficiency of villages did not mean that every village was far away and separate from the neighbouring villages or that each village in its habitat lived a life of splendid isolation from the rest of the world. In an age of interdependence no village could cut itself away from the main stream of national life. This is absolutely essential for the all round progress and prosperity of the villages, which is a key unit at grass roots level in a nation. "My idea of village swaraj", (says Gandhi"), is a complete republic, independent of its neighbours for its vital wants, and yet interdependent for, many others in which dependence is a necessity".[18]

In Gandhi's concept of village swaraj every village must be freedom of manage its affairs without external interference from above in its area of competence. It must have its own organisational structure in the form of Government. Gandhi held the view that "the Government of the village will be conducted by the Panchayat of five members, annually elected by the adult villagers, male and female, possessing minimum prescribed qualifications......... Since there will be no system of punishments in the accepted sense, this panchayat will be the legislature, judiciary, and executive combined to operate for its year of office. Any village can become such a republic today without much interference even from the present Government".[19]

In essence, the panchayat of every village republic, is a key unit for decentralisation of legislative, executive and judicial powers. Every village with its characteristics of self-rule and self-sufficiency is supposed to represent the values of a true democracy, where in authority and power are shared and exercised by different functionaries. The individual will have complete freedom to shape his destiny according to his wishes. His thoughts and actions will be pervaded by the spirit of non-violence in an atmosphere of genuine freedom. The spirit of self-sacrifice and patriotism will be the mainspring of all constructive actions in such a village republic. Gandhi argued that in such a setting it was, possible to secure "perfect democracy".... based upon individual freedom. The individual is the architect of his own Government. The law of non-violence rules him and his Government..... For the law governing every village is that he will suffer death in the defence of his and his village's honour".[20]

In the modern world, though different nations prefers different ideologies like democracy, communism etc.: one similarity in almost every nation of the world is the pyramid structure of the administrative system. Normally, it is known and accepted by one and all that power flows from top to bottom rather than the other way around. But Gandhi's greatest contribution was to alter fundamentally the base, structure and shape of the power pyramid. In his scheme of village swaraj the pivotal element is the individual who comes into his own. After that comes the village, and finally group of villages. Decentralisation of power is possible in a structure consisting of a large number of different villages encompassing each other in concentric circles. The Gandhian power pyramid structure operates on the assumption that human beings as individual entitles are capable of carving out their own destinies, without interference or coercion from the functionaries at the top. Gandhi believed that in such an oceanic circle the individual will rise to the occasion and be prepared to sacrifice everything for the cause his village.[21] Under such a decentralised structure governing rural India, "the outermost circumference will not wield power to crush the inner circle but give strength to all within and derives its own from the centre. If there ever is to be a republic of everything in India, then I claim variety for my picture in which the last is equal to the first, or in other words none is to be the first and none the last".[22]

Gandhi took a whole some picture of the socio-economic and political conditions in India. His insight into these problems were based on a close study, and an understanding born out of practical wisdom. He began with village swaraj and ended up in proposing Ramraj or enlightened anarchy through the instrumentality of non-violence. Gandhi was in search of an ideal state where everyone was his own ruler without much interference by the state. As a realist

Gandhi had his own doubts whether the ultimate goal of Ramraj would come about in India in his own life time.[23]

If effect, the exalted values like non-violence, individual freedom and equality have given a solid base to Gandhi's concept of decentralisation of power at the political level. In addition to this consideration of his concept of Swaraj, in which the panchayat was to function as the basic unit of the Government for bringing about self-sufficiency, constitutes an integral element of a purely decentralised democracy.

Economic Decentralisation

Gandhi was not a professional economist in the true sense of the term. But in a large and eventful life he had occasion to develop his economic ideas based on the situation in India. Gandhian economic theory provides a new and realistic approach to contemporary problems of poverty, hunger and degradation. Beginning with the position that exploitation is at the root of all violence, Gandhi builds his economic ideas in such a manner that avoids exploitation of man by man. His panacea is to do away with concentration of economic power by proposing economic decentralisation at various levels of the power hierarchy of the Indian society. Gandhi frequently asserted that "if India is to evolve along non-violent lines, it will have to decentralise many things".[24]

Gandhiji firmly believed that mechanised economy model is no longer a valid model and salvation of masses lies in a decentralised organic economy. A centralised economy leads to the concentration of population in the cities, leading to many problems of urbanisation. Gangsterism, alienation from society and natural surroundings leading to slums, pollution of the atmosphere, problems of housing and water supply, acceptance of material values as against spiritual, violence and crime and many other social vices are its natural consequences. Centralisation has caused inequalities among the people conflicting interests, warring classes, wasteful competition dehumanised market, over production of luxuries and harmful articles, while the basic needs are not satisfied and the degradation of skilled workers. It is due to centralisation that Western Europe though the colonial exploitation of the countries of Asia, Africa and Latin America began an era of rapid and sustained economic growth which culminated in the creation of the contemporary world characterised by a "Great Divide" between the rich countries comprising of the nations of Western Europe, North America and the poor countries of Asia, Africa and Latin America. Gandhi's economic critique of imperialism is non-marxist in origin tracing back the influences of Naoroji, Ruskin, Gokhale and Tolstoy. Centralised economy has created disparity to the extent that today the industrial countries account for less than 30 percent of world population. Yet they consume more than 80 percent of world production. All but few metals will be exhausted within 50 years, if consumption rates continue to grow as they are.[25] The effulgent and the wastes of industrial life poison the atmosphere and the seas with consequent hazards to the health of plants, birds, fish and men. In the United States altogether cars, factories and homes put 140 million tons of pollution in to the atmosphere each year or about three fourths of a ton for every man, woman and child.[26] The spiritual and moral erosion on account of swallowing centralisation was apprehended even at the time of the rise of mechanised economy by Carlyle, Ruskin Dickens and Goldsmith. However, even the protagonists of decentralisation assign definite place for large scale centralised key industries, making use of the latest technology to produce sophisticated items but there should be no doubt that in a country like India having immense man power the decentralised sector has got to be the dominant sector.

Gandhi Ji visualises a decentralised economic order where there would be no exploitation social or economic of man by man. Generally decentralisation is viewed as pronounced priority to the small scale and cottage industries but the concept of decentralization in fact is all pervading.

Gandhi Ji had advocated several times in favour of decentralised development of the country. He favoured decentralisation in economic as well as political area. He was totally against the centralised efforts. He rightly felt that we have been dazzled by the material achievements of highly industrialised societies in the west and have blindly followed their lead ignoring the differences in social, political and economic conditions prevailing in our country. The development based on labour-saving machines led to the mass production in a centralised way and the distribution also is resorted to in that manner. It has helped in the development of such a society where the gap between the "haves" and "have-nots" has increased tremendously. It also helped in the extensive use of machines in such a manner which resulted in making the machine of the men and displacing large number of people from the employment. The Industrial Revolution, as it took place in the western countries, helped in gradually reducing the hours of work in the factories so that the men could be received from the drudgery of the work and the human existence may be made more enjoyable with leisure and means to enjoy it. But Gandhiji had a different idea on this issue. He felt that "the problem with us is now how to find leisure for the teeming millions inhabiting our villages but the problem is how to utilize their idle hours which are equal to the working days of six months in a year. It has been rightly pointed out that "it is only when there is decentralisation of the production of basic needs of people and limited reliance on centralised industry that all other postulates of Gandhian economic order can function".[27] Gandhi advocated of village self-sufficiency so that the villagers could no remain dependent upon others, at least for their needs.

Production on mass scale with the help of machines in a centralised manner has not solved our basic problems of unemployment and poverty. It has, in fact, aggravated this problem as we find it today, specially in our country. We all know that with the centralised planning and wide use of large scale industrialization, we have not been able to solve these problems in our country. The backlog of unemployed people has been on the increase and poverty is still rampant.

According to Gandhiji decentralistion is one of the means to create classless, unexploited and egalitarian society. The word decentralised sector in economics is used to refer to the cottage industries located in the rural areas. But in fact the Gandhian concept of decentralisation is related to the rural economy as a whole. It is pervasive to the Gandhian concept of economic philosophy technical progress, emphasis on agriculture and tiny sector, co-operatives, distributive justice, employment mixed economy, barter system, villagism and the doctrine of trusteeship and rural transformation of Indian economy etc. Gandhian concept towards decentralization contains the key for reshaping the existing pattern of our social, political and economic systems. When Gandhiji used the terms khadi, village industries, Swadeshi and the like he meant decentralisation of production and direct co-relation between consumption, production and utilisation of locally available resources. In the economic field Mahatma was in favour of "Production by masses" in place of the modern craze for mass production. To my mind in the economic field the doctrine of decentralisation implies that the economic system - production and distribution growth with social justice so that the benefits trickle down to the millions of masses.

All over the world, some of the best brains of the age were thinking in terms quite akin to that of decentralisation pluralism, regionalism, syndicatism, guild socialism fabianism, anarchism and the movements for Municipal rule in the U.S. all these to revivify life in small groups and localities. Anarchists thinkers, Proudhon, Bakunin and Kropotkin advocated voluntary federalism of autonomous communes life in which will be broadly surveyable.[28]

Theory of Technical progress

Gandhiji wanted that man should not be subservient to technology, rather technology should remain controlled in the service of man, to reduce him drudgery and to help solve his material problems. Gandhi's views on machinery and by extension on innovations, inventions and technology were apart of the whole which included values, institutions and indeed the whole culture and as a fore runner he attached enormous importance to the culture and value impact of technology and he linked it with society, economy, justice and positive decision making. Indeed a Gandhian view of technology outside the scope of economy, social justice and its impacts on man's value system simply does not exist. He did not treat technology as neutral nor as an exogenous element. He was definitely opposed to technological determinism. As he says, "what I object is the craze for machinery not machinery as such. The craze is for what they call labour saving machinery. Men go on" saving labour" till thousands are without work and thrown on the open street to die to starvation".[29]

We know that Gandhiji was not against the use of machines or centralisation wherever it was indispensable. He was not opposed to machines as such but he was not against making men slaves of machines. He was against it as it concentrates production and distribution in the hands of a few. He very well knew that this body itself is a most delicate piece of machine. What he objected to was the craze for machine. He stated that I am not against machinery as such, but I am opposed to it when it masters us."[30] He was thus practical enough to realise that machinery cannot be discarded totally. He, therefore, explained that "I am aiming not at eradication of all machinery but its limitation". He further pointed out that " My machinery must be of the most elementary type which I can put in the homes of the millions". He objected to the use of machinery as an instrument of greed and approved of any machine which does not deprive masses of men of the opportunity to labour but which helps the individual and add to his efficiency and which a man can handle at will without being its slave".[31]

Modern man seems to be attracted by violent technology while non-violent and soft technology repels him. But of late even in the west there is a trend towards intermediate technology and every where there is realization that Labour saving, capital intensive, highly sophisticated technology transfer of mass production has no relevance to the "Third world where there is plenty of labour, little capital, lack of technical sophistication and elaborate infrastructure. The task of the future, for rich and poor alike is to develop non-violent technologies. Systematic work to create non-violent technologies was started some 22 years ago by a London group of professionals under the title "Intermediate Technology Development" which has attracted increasing interest also from the advanced countries. "Intermediate Technology emphasis four criteria" Non-violence, smallness, simplicity and cheapness. Dr. Ernst Schumucher, a former chief Economic Adviser to Britians National Coal Board and the founder of the Intermediate Technology group, in his recent publication entitled "Small is Beautiful" has lent unqualified support to "appropriate or middle technology.

Production, Distribution, Consumption and Exchange and Employment

The Gandhian Concept of decentralisation and planning is reflected in his views on production, distribution, consumption and exchange. The Mahatma was in favour of "Production by masses" in place of the modern craze for "mass production". He favoured participative growth with social justice so that the benefits of production may trickle down to the millions of masses. The Mahatma favoured an appropriate middle technology which would help augment agricultural and industrial production for raising the per capita productivity without throwing people out of employment. Gandhi's concern for employment crystallised in his statement on the eve of independence on the purpose of planning as "real planing consisted in the best utilization of the whole man power of India". In the Gandhian scheme emphasis is laid on self-employment.

The whole programme of Mahatma Gandhi is built on the solid foundations of economic equality and distributive justice which never means possession of an equal amount of worldly goods by everyone. It means that every one will have proper house to live, sufficient and balanced food to eat and sufficient Khadi to cover himself. Gandhiji ceaselessly talked of meeting the basic needs of food, clothing and shelter for the last man of India. But equal distribution was not to be confused with crude equality. "The real implication of equal distribution is that each man shall have the where withal to supply all his natural needs and no more. To bring this ideal into being the entire social order has got to be reconstructed. A society based on non-violence cannot nature any other social ideal".[32] Gandhiji asserted "The possession of inordinate wealth by individuals should be held as a crime against Indian humanity".[33] He further observes "My ideal is equal distribution, but so far as I can see it is not to be realised. I therefore work for equitable distribution".[34]

Mahatma's thinking about consumption was derived from his definition of civilization, his faith in redistribution as well as his commitment to the ideal of non-possession which god seekers must purpose. An aesthetically and hedonistically luxurious life was alien to the Gandhian ethos. As Gandhi says "He (who has made the ideal of equal distribution a part of his being) world reduce his wants to a minimum, bearing in mind the poverty in India".[35] According to Gandhiji 'civilization in the real sense of the term, consists not in the multiplication of wants but in their deliberate and voluntary restrictions".[36]

In his ideal of "villagism", Gandhiji advocated barter system. Bapu was conscious of the blessings of money and the importance of monetary policy but he was equally apprehensive of the veil, peril and confusion that results from the dominance of money. In the Gandhian economy labour is the coin which may be bartered for any material things. When his self-sufficient village needs something which it cannot produce, it can easily exchange with the produce which has been grown in abundance at another place. Thus Gandhiji envisaged that trade will be the barter system. When objected that this is a revision to the primitive system of barter, Gandhiji replied "Is not all international trade based on the barter system ?[37] On the whole the Gandhian view on technology, employment, growth and social justice is neatly expressed in the passage. "I want to save time and labour, not for a fraction of man kind, but for all. I want the concentration of wealth not in the hands of a few, but in the hands of all. Today machinery helps the few to ride on the backs of the millions. The impetus behind it is not the philanthropy to save labour but greed. It is against this constitution of thing that I am fighting with all my might".[38]

Gandhi' new theory of trusteeship was put forth to remove the wide disparity between the rich and the hungry millions.[39] He said that he would personally prefer decentralisation of power from the hands of the state, through an emphasis on trusteeship.[40] He also believed that trusteeship could bring about a non-violent state. A harmonious relationship between labour and capital could merge out of a trusteeship theory that placed emphasis on a balanced relationship between the rich and the poor.

Trusteeship means all money and property originally belongs to society and those who are possessing it are only the trustees of the society whose duty is to increase the earning and value of the trust property. He should charge only that much from the trust property as is absolutely essential for his subsistence and honorable living. Excess of one's income over and above one's livings is a social surplus to be employed for the benefit of the society. Breach of trust is a crime and is punishable under law.[41] Under the trusteeship theory of Gandhi certain limited property rights are admissible. The Trusteeship theory of Gandhi does not recognise the inherent, unrestricted, irresponsible and absolute right of private property. Possession of private property such as family farms, small business, family dwellings etc., which confers freedom and independence upon the owners without causing in any manner exploitation of other members of society, is admissible under this theory and should be permitted and encouraged by society, for its natural operation, growth and development. Such possession of private property will not be tainted and it will not be an insolent demonstration of inequalities. Big landed estates and big business capital should be brought to co-operative ownership or diversified public ownership to check the concentration of economic power. The theory envisages trusteeship of legitimately and fairly acquired money and property and not that of the ill-gotten wealth acquired from exploitation of others. In this doctrine Gandhiji emphasised on economic equality. Gandhiji held the view that "the rich cannot accumulate wealth without the co-operation of the poor in the society".[42] His trusteeship theory involved the transfer of accumulated private wealth to community ownership, where labourers and peasants are co-partners with capitalists and land lord. Through trusteeship every individual would be able to get sufficient work to enable him to provide his daily requirements. Such an ideal could be universally realised if the means of production of basic necessities of life could remain under the control of the masses.[43] The production by the masses could be followed by equitable distribution of the produced goods. Gandhi puts forth his theory of trusteeship on the assumption that economic power should be in the hands of the community, wherein each member is responsible to produce his needs and to own wealth and property of the community for the welfare of the society.

Non-possession and bread-labour are two other concepts of Gandhi. Non-possession meant not having food or anything beyond immediate need and bread labour meant that every man should labour with his body for his food and clothing. These two concepts could go along way in bringing about dignity of labour in every human being. Gandhian economic thought is conceived in the basic necessities of life, where each person should work with his own body to fulfil his needs. In his novel theory of trusteeship Gandhi sought to transfer power from the state to the trusteeship of the community at large.

The trusteeship theory may not be relevant in a society characterised by heavy emphasis on material aspects of life. However, if the trusteeship theory is put into practice it can become a major instrument for decentralisation of economic power for the greatest welfare of the people in the society.

Gandhi's ideas have suffered considerably due to over simplification and distortion by writers who take a deterministic view of his theory. Gandhi's genius was too vast to be amenable to any rigid schematic classification. He was a conservative and revolutionary and realist and Utopian. Gandhi did not leave a specific body of knowledge or theories for he had not systematically worked out all the details of his theories or concepts so as to make them internally consistent. His ideas at best could be regarded as congeries of concepts, norms, values, principles and propositions. There was never any finality in Gandhian thinking while formulating theories or concepts. This was the case because Gandhi very rarely conceived his theories or propositions which were not closely related to time and place. Gandhi's ideas frequently underwent change as he was always conducting one experiment or the other.[44]

If the Gandhian approach for the development of economy on a decentralisation way is adopted, it would also need a change in the present system of education and training. Much of the cost of education and training would be reduced considerably and would not go waste as we find it today. Crores of students are wasting their time, energy and money for getting a kind of education which they find to be quite useless. This has been causing great anxiety and frustration for them. The restlessness of the society on this account is also quite marked and politicians with vested interests are taking political advantage out of it. The students are being exploited too for the selfish gains of a few. If we make efforts to train the youth of the villages with simple arts and crafts so that they may do something to earn their living by staying in the villages itself we would be doing more service to them rather than attracting them in the urban centres with all their glamour and out moded system of education meant only for making them clerks in the offices. We all know that simple arts and crafts may be learnt within a few months at much limited cost and time. We should teach them to learn things themselves and understand the intricacies and fineness of the life, their cultural values and better and decent way of living. They should be explained the importance of dignity of labour, simple living and high thinking. They should be explained about our cultural heritage and how to preserve it without training them to love foreign culture and foreign goods more and more. This will also help in hastening the process of decentralisation in the country.

If we do not follow the approach of decentralised development in the country as advocated by Gandhiji the dignity of man as a man also is lowered considerably.

Gandhiji's concept of decentralisation is the product of his wide ranging mind which probed into the harsh realities of man's social, political and economic life. From a wider perspective it can be said that Gandhi through his concept of decentralisation was trying to find solutions to certain basic issues like arbitrary state power, unlimited violence, economic exploitation of man by man, removal of poverty and socio-economic inequalities.

References

1. Quoted in Ved Mehta, Mahatma Gandhi and His Apostles, London, Andre Deutsch Ltd., 1977, p.3.
2. Shriman Narayan, India Needs Gandhi, New Delhi, S. Chand and Co. Pvt. Ltd., 1976, p.1.
3. Harijan, March 14, 1936, p. 37.
4. Harijan, June 24, 1939, p. 174.
5. Harijan, Sept. 7, 1935, p. 234.
6. The Modern Review, Oct. 1935, p. 413.
7. Ibid.
8. Harijan, March 9, 1940, p. 31.
9. Young India, March 2, 1981, p.5.
10. Harijan, June 18, 1942, p.5.
11. Harijan, Feb, 11, 1939, p.8.
12. Harijan, Jan. 18, 1942, p.5.
13. Quoted in Gopinath Dhawan, The political philosophy of Mahatma Gandhi, Ahmedabad, Navjivan Publishing House, 1946, p. 282.
14. Young India, July 2, 1931, p. 162.
15. V.P. Verma, The political philosophy of Mahtama Gandhi and Sarvodaya, Agra, Laxmi Narain Agarwal, 1965, p. 278.
16. V.P. Verma, "The Philosophical and sociological foundations of Gandhism", Gandhian concept of state, (Ed. by), B.B. Majumdar, Calcutta, M.C. Shankar and sons, 1957, pp. 79-80.
17. Young India, Vol. III, p. 547.
18. Harijan, July 26, p. 238.
19. Ibid.
20. Ibid.
21. M.K. Gandhi, Panchayat Raj, Ahmedabad, Navjivan Publishing

House, 1959, pp. 8-10.

22. M.K. Gandhi, Ibid, pp. 8-10.
23. Quoted in J.N. Lal, "Gandhian Democracy and Its Relevance", in the Relevance of Gandhi to our Times, New Delhi, R. Achuthan, Secretary, Committee for National and International Seminars of the National Committee for the Gandhi Centenary, 1970, p. 146.
24. Harijan, Dec, 30, 1939, p. 391.
25. Edward Goldsmith and others:- A Blue print for survival, Town Stacey, London, 1972.

    Also:- Robert L. Heil Broner" -Growth and Survival" in Foreign Affairs Vol. 51, No. 1.
26. Ruth Moore:- Man in the Environment, Alfred, A. Kuopt, N.Y., 1975.
27. Mathur J.S. Industrial civilization- A Gandhian view point compiled in Industrial civilization and Gandhian Economics, Pustakayan, Allahabad, p. 26.
28. J.S. Bains, (Ech.):- Studies in political science, Asia 1961, pp. 249-50.
29. Young India, November 13, 1924, pp. 85-86.
30. Harijan, 1937, p. 18.
31. Ram K. Vepa :- New Technology: A Gandhian concept, p. 99.
32. Louis Fischer:- The Life of Mahatma Gandhi, p. 356.
33. Raj Krishna:- Voluntary Action, Sept. 1978, Vol. XX, No. 9,p.7.
34. Ibid.
35. Ibid.
36. Ibid, p.8.
37. M.K. Gandhi : Harijan, 2 November, 1934.
38. Mahadeo Desai: In Defence of Machinery "Young India", June 22, 1935, pp. 91-92.
39. M.K. Gandhi, constructive programme: Its meaning and place, Ahmedabad, Navjivan press, 1944, p.18.
40. See B.S. Sharma, Gandhi as a pollitical Thinker, Allahabad, Indian Press Pvt. Ltd., 1956, p. 138.
41. M.K. Gandhi : Young India, April 24, 1937.
42. B.S. Sharma, Gandhi as a political Thinker, Allahabad, Indian Press Pvt. Ltd., 1956, p. 138.
43. Young India, III, pp. 923-24.
44. C.V. Raghavalu and R. Anandarao, "Gandhi-An approach to Decentralisation : Its Relevance", The Indian Journal of Public Administration, Vol. XXIV, NO. 3, July-Sept; 1978, pp. 710-722.

6
Gandhian Approach to Rural Industrialization

In this chapter an attempt is made to assess the prospects of change in the present socio-economic structure of rural areas on Gandhian path of rural industrialization.

GANDHIJI had, through his far-reaching constructive programme drawn the attention of the nation on the said plight of rural-fold. As such, since independence, much stress is being given on the development of rural areas of this country. So far, the programme of rural transformation was based on the Keynesian doctrine of monetary and fiscal regulations. It was thought that the general economic development of the country could be so expansive as to include rural transformation within its scope. By assuming that rural industrialization would be a resultant phenomenon of the percolation effect of metropolitan industrialisation, Indian planners ignored the need for evolving any special approach to the problem. But the strategy adopted for rural development has failed to satisfy the aspirations of the village people. These plans have not yielded must benefit to the rural folk inhabiting our hundreds of millions of villages. The economic benefits of progress and development have not reached the remote villages and the weaker sections of our society. Our villagers still face the difficulties even in obtaining the basic necessities of life, like drinking water facilities for all, education, medical and health services and communication. The crisis in the Indian villages, simmering for the last 45 years, has now attained a perilous dimension. In order to improve the situation, a radically different approach to rural development is needed.

In India where there are different type of practical in regard to social, political and economic orders as against those found in the Western countries, the Gandhian approach to rural development and rural industrialization has more relevance in the present context than the modern economic thought.

Since majority of the people in our country life in villages, the unit of development in Gandhian technique was the village itself. "Identifying himself with India's poor, he turned the thoughts of the nation to the needs for rural millions for whom "life was an eternal compulsory fast", who "live because they can not die at will". Hence he visualized that, 'the development of the country lies in the development of the rural masses and rural areas". This is because, they are the backbone of the country".[1]

Gandhian strategy for rural development includes the development of the village and small scale industries, village handicrafts, development of agriculture, improvement of rural health, education and sanitation, betterment of the backward communities, specially Harijans democratic decentralization of rural development, even distribution of income, wealth and co-operation at all levels accordingly.

Since time immemorial, villages provides the base for the economic structure of the country while towns produced more sophisticated articles. The industrial structure was thus well diversified and dispersed. It was the British who destroyed not only our glorious trade but also our rural industries in self-interest. The industrial revolution of England thrived at the cost of India, while the artisans of the country were wiped out from the industrial scene. The basic contradiction of modern industrial civilization was very well diagnosed by Mahatma Gandhi. The goal of rural-urban integration under which land management is better organized to support industrialization for bridging the productivity gap between rural and urban workers might be an ideal where the cultural fusion between the two societies is complete. Under existing Indian conditions, according to Gandhi, "We shall have to find out whether the villager who produces an article or foodstuff rests content with exporting it and with using a cheap substitute imported from outside. We shall have to see that the villagers become first of all self-contained and then cater for the needs of the city dwellers".[2] Till Gandhiji enunciated his view villages were looked upon as appendages to the towns Gandhiji wanted to reverse the process. According to Gandhiji, a healthy economic relationship between town and country implies the fulfilment of the following interrelated conditions "(i) that in the rural economy of his conception cities must find their "natural place" in the economy, (ii) that they must primarily be 'clearing houses' for the village products; (iii) that the primary of agriculture, and of industries allied to agriculture, in the rural areas, should be recognized as the foundation of economic development; and (iv) that the economic relation between town and country must be reciprocally beneficial not exploitative".[3]

What we have now to change, therefore, is the faulty economic thinking which made the big industrial plants the focus of development, and the elitist attitude to the problem of masses. It is here that, more than any other figure in our history, Gandhian concept is of relevance today. I am far from suggesting that Gandhi's solution to Indian poverty are to be accepted merely because it came from him. But it will be suicidal to overlook Gandhiji in the face of the fact that India would progress only if its villages are made self-contained and self-sufficient, and that our planning has not helped to achieve and objective.

A self-contained village according to Gandhi had immense possibilities for growth, but difficulty arises in defining a unit which could be considered self-contained, Gandhi thought that an area covered by a radius of eight kilometers could be considered the basic unit, of which the centre was not fixed. Each individual of the family could also in a way be considered the centre of such units. Each basic unit would have a natural consumption pattern depending upon its geology, physiological and temperamental conditions of the people, their customs and traditions, occupational pattern and economic undertaking, and educational and cultural attainments. These factors determine the mode of living of the community and therefore its consumption requirements and pattern of consumption. In self-contained basic units the well integrated production plans would necessarily be linked with natural consumption requirements of the region, and production would essentially be restricted and guided by the resources locally available. The schedule of production possibilities of an area would be drawn on the basis of the available local resources keeping in view the natural requirement of the locality. On a close integration of the schedule of production possibility and natural consumption pattern, according to Gandhiji, depended on the self-generating growth potential of the rural community. Otherwise it could be vulnerable to urban exploitation, which in fact, has occurred during the last few decades.

The new movement under various guises of appropriate technology is in fact a revival of the Gandhian approach to ideal rural organization based on the integration of its natural consumption pattern and the schedule of its production possibility. And it is only in this Gandhian approach that the panacea of rural crisis lies.

The problem of unemployment, specially the disguised one, poses a serious problem in rural areas in Indian and it is the basic cause for rural poverty. We require dynamic plan to use the vendable dynamo of human energy which can become a moving devil. Vast masses of men cannot remain without work. Gandhiji said " Swaraj has no meaning for the million if they do not know how to employ their enforced idleness. To a people famishing and idle, the only acceptable form in which God can dare appear is work and promise of food as wages. God created man to work for his food, and said that those who are without work were thieves. Eighty per cent of Indians are compulsorily thieves half the year". He continued, " I have found it impossible to soothe suffering patients with a song from Kabir. The hungry millions ask for one poem-invigorating food. They cannot be given it. They must earn it. And they can earn only by the sweat of their brow".[4]

Gandhiji explained this problem vividly in the following words, "Imagine therefore what a calamity it must be to have 300 million unemployed several millions becoming degraded every day for want of employment devoid of self respect, devoid of faith in God, I dare not take them the message of God. I can take before them a message of God only by taking the message of sacred work before them. It is good enough to talk of God whilst we are sitting here after a nice breakfast...."[5] Under these circumstances people and sometimes nations come to lose their confidence in peaceful change through democratic and non-violent means and so become desperate and opt to resort to force.

In a developing country like India with its large population and rather restricted amount of capital at its disposal it is in all reality an Herculean task to provide full employment to its citizens, without undertaking industrial decentralization on a very wide scale throughout the country side. This can be possible, as Gandhiji said only through the establishment of small scale, cottage and village industries. Gandhiji's thought identifies economic development with the preservation of the small producer and its participation in a diversified pattern of productive activity. For Gandhi the small producer is both the subject as well as the object of economic development. Economic development is meaningful only if it is aimed at lifting up the small peasant and artisan economy from the state of pauperism and despair and at converting the small producer himself into an active force in productive activity. Gandhi seems to suggest that industrialisation of the Western type will achieve neither of these two objectives in India. It is not likely to lift up the small producer from the state of pauperism nor is likely to draw him into the fold of expanding productive activity. In fact, western type of development is bound to result in vast social tension and political turmoil as it would hit the small producers which constitute the most numerous section in Indian society. The identification of the small producer as the key element of the Indian society and the definition of the Indian development in terms of the welfare of this vast mass of working humanity constitute Gandhiji's signal contributions to thinking on Indian development.[6] Dr. Ropke after referring to the doubtful standard of material prosperity of masses as an object in under-developed countries to be attained said, 'it is regrettable that India seems to follow materialist socialism rather than Gandhi's ideas to the present programme of economic development".[7]

There are a number of villages and cottage industries which can be developed with advantages. Among the number of village industries mention may be made of processing of cereals and pulses, ghani oil, villages leather, cottage match, manufacturer of cane gur and khandsari, palm gurmaking and other products, non-edible oils and soaps, hand made paper, beekeeping, village pottery fibre, carpentry and black smithy, lime manufacturing, gobar gas, collection of forest plants and fruits for medicinal purposes, schellac, manufacturing of gums and resins, manufacture of khatha, food processing and food preservation, bamboo and cane work, manufacture of household aluminum utensils and khadi. These industries enable the villages to develop local initiative, co-operation and a spirit of self-reliance. They also help utilisation of the available manpower for processing the locally available raw materials by adoption of simple techniques. These industries have capacity to correct the regional imbalances by initiating industrial activities an dispersed basis in the most neglected, backward and inaccessible areas, where perhaps large scale sector is unable to penetrate. Another striking feature is that, as compared to the organized sector, there is no element of exploitation or profiteering, the wage content of the prices at which these products are sold is relatively higher compared to that of similar products manufactured in all organized sector. In short such rural industry could provide employment, increase incomes, slow down migration to cities and increase the supply of goods and services to farmers at lower cost and generally stimulate rural and regional development. Looking from all points of view, the development of village industries can be an effective solution to many of the problems that confront us today.

Gandhiji was always laying great stress on khadi and village industries. In fact, he have a place of honour to spinning. As Gandhiji said, "Khadi is the sun of the village solar system. The planets are the various industries which can support khadi in return for the heat and the substance they derive from it".[8] He was happy that the 'Charkha' was a simple machine which would bring solace to the poverty-stricken people. He felt that without the spinning wheel there was no swaraj. If Gandhiji pleaded for Khadi, he was not being just a romantic idealist. In fact, he listed all its advantages and then asked his critics to suggest any other alternative occupation to the millions who are punished with forced idleness for six months of the year. "Do not make the majority of your countrymen as compulsory thieves"[9] he pleaded for in his view anyone who eats without working is a thief. "My sole claim for khadi" he had written "is that it offers an immediate, practicable and permanent solution to the twin problems of enforced idleness and chronic starvation".[10] His arguments, as always, are bold, logical unemotional and unassiable. It is no argument to dub his scheme as old fashioned, unless something at least as effective is suggested and so far this has not been done.

While he stressed the multiplier effect on employment of concurrent development of a wide range of village industries, Gandhi did not forget to emphasize the importance of (a) quality, and (b) cost-consciousness and efficiency of production. As regards quality,

Gandhiji was right when he referred to the degradation to taste brought about by the cheap and tardy imported products of foreign manufacture. While admiring works of Indian fold-at in an exhibition in 1936. Gandhi said: 'Our tastes have been so debased that the miracles happening before our own eyes appear like so much dust or clay and trifles from abroad became exquisite peaces of art, water from a spring in far off Europe with the witchery of an unintelligible name becomes invested with a miraculous quality".[11] Thus it was not always rational consumers' preference that queered the pitch for the Indian handicrafts. Their products, though aesthetically superior, had lost their traditional attractiveness for the consumer. But through long neglect workmanship had also deteriorated in quality. Gandhi, therefore, said; "We must induce the village craftsmen to improve their workmanship and not dismiss them because foreign or even articles produced in cities, i.e., big factories, are superior. In this way we shall repay somewhat the debt we owe to them. We must mentally go back to the villages and treat them as our pattern, instead of putting the city life before them for imitation".[12] Gandhiji was aware of the wastes of Khadi production. He said, "so far we have simply tried to manufacture khadi for the city people. The producer must wear khadi. Cost can thus be reduced."[13] Overheads were too high. The middlemen had still to be eliminated. Gandhiji thought that, since there was a limit to the improvement in technology, there had to be utmost cost reduction in other ways.

One feels confident that a comprehensive and well-integrated programme of rural electrification, development and extension credit and marketing facilities, technical and research and assistance, supply of improved machinery and equipment, extension of training facilities, etc. would surely assist the industrialization of rural areas and provide gainful opportunities for employment in the rural areas. At the same time such development will also provide solution to other socio-economic problems such as halting the exodus of rural population to urban centres, diversification of occupations and raising incomes, and thus standard of living in rural communities.

The principal task in rural industrialisation is the organization of rural industries. The task of organisation includes disseminating advanced know how to the rural artisans, supply of raw materials and collection of finished products for marketing. The mass illiteracy in India has seriously hampered the development of co-operative mode of organization. The illiterate villagers are quite ignorant of the principle of management of a co-operative organization. Thus, for a long time the rural artisans will need to be spoon-fed in the field of organization by Government and other public institutions. Perhaps the biggest snag in rural industrialization is that agro-based industries task, therefore, is to strengthen the organizational effort in the rural areas and to make the managers and accountants of the registered institutions and the co-operative societies much more socially accountable than many of them would like to be or they have been so far. The point is often missed that the programme for village industries has to implemented in the context of the existing national situation and not in a void.[14]

The development of village industries would not only solve the problem of rural unemployment but also enable us to balance our occupational pattern. Revitalization of our rural areas in every way is the only answer to change favourably our occupations structure. We have to provide not only primary amenities such as good water, clean roads, electricity education and health centres but also fuller gainful employment to the working population in the diversified rural economy, besides agriculture. Against the backdrop of this reality the development of village industries, therefore, assumes significance. The aim of the Government policy, should, therefore be as Gandhiji observed nearly half a century ago to "return to the villages the industries that have been cruelly and thought-lessly snatched away from them by the city dwellers".

It should be reiterated that Gandhi's concept of economic decentralisation for economic growth in the form of small and home industries does not in any way oppose the use of science and technology which could develop the village and cottage industries. What Gandhiji wanted to achieve through the revival of village and cottage industries was to utilize the enormous capacity of the nation which was going waste. Once it was accomplished he would have been only too glad to adopt all the modern methods of supplementary knowledge and technique for increasing production. "How can I be against machinery when I know that even this body is the most delicate machine. The supreme consideration is man. The machine should not make atrophied the limbs of man"[15] he argued. He was in favour of every machine that improves the efficiency and productivity and lightens the burden of the artisan and the cottage worker. "My machinery must be of the most elementary type which I can put in the home of the millions".[16] Even under this decentralized system there will be need for some large scale industries. To quote him, "....I am socialist enough to say that such factories should be nationalised, or state-controlled. They ought only to be working under the most attractive and ideal conditions not for profit, but for the benefit of humanity, love taking the place of greed as motive. It is an alteration in the conditions of labour that I want. This mad rush for wealth must cease, and the labourer must be assured not only a living wage, but a daily task that is not a mere drudgery".[17] His aim was at limiting the use of machinery to the extent where they cease to help the individual and begin to encroach upon his individuality. Gandhiji had said " it is only when the machine has been put into its proper places can we think of non-violence. "Gandhiji maintained that there should be ample scope for decentralisation of industry, and economic and social power, under the nonviolent pattern of economic planning. Gandhiji desired that the fullest initiative must lie in the hands of the rural communities that they experiences"[18] a glow of freedom "through self-half and self-reliance. This was the reason why he was so keen on developing the Indian village panchayat system as an integral part of the future economic and political organisation of the country. I do not think any modern economist could find fault with this clear enunciation of Gandhian views regarding the policy of mechanization in developing countries in India. Prof. Gunnar Myrdal has strongly supported Gandhi's emphasis on villages and cottage industries because "South Asian countries now run the risk of creating petty island of highly organized western type industries that will remain surrounded by a sea of stagnation". Prof. Myrdal observed, "The development of industries in direct competition with existing cottage industries would take work and bread away from millions with no immediate alternative source of employment or income. This would not be rational from a planning point of view ...... As there is no prospect of any large scale adjustment for decades to come, particularly as the labour force will increase rapidly until the end of the century".[19]

The dynamic balance between 'Man' and 'Machine' which Gandhiji and intuitively sensed as necessary is now accepted by most thinkers as the only possible approach for a really productive efforts. Japan had demonstrated in the last 112 years that it is the optimum 'man-machine' mix that can significantly raise productivity which in turn has been responsible for its phenomenal growth, often termed, a 'miracle'. In India, too, it is being realised that what is needed in the rural sector for quick results is an 'appropriate technology' that would match the skills and resources available in the area and that this would have to be tailored to meet the actual situations instead of indiscriminate import from the West.

Gandhiji was in favour of developing a technology which did not create articulate value system for the society but could harmonise with the existing culture. In order to bring this orientation, we have to boost our way of developing programmes in our laboratories which must be relevance and interaction with the people and their dire needs. We have to work at the lines of technology with raw materials, social needs, people's skills etc.

We must think in terms of reviving old technology or adopt a current one or inventing a new one, or improving the traditional 'indigenous technology'. It would be better to switch over to 'intermediate technology' a technology somewhere between 'the advanced the backward' . In India, to quote Prof. Gadgils "the backward may be identified with the technology of traditional Indian industry and the 'advanced', with the technology of the industrially advanced countries.[20] Schumacher observes, "Intermediate technology would be vastly superior in productivity to their traditional technology while at the same time being vastly cheaper and simpler than the highly sophisticated and enormous capital intensive technology of the west. As a general guide it may be said that this 'Intermediate technology' should be on the level of £70 to £100 equipment cost per average work place". He concedes that there are certain sectors and localities in every developing country which are irrevocably committed to the western technology, but, for the rest of the economy he suggested a technology that should fulfill four requirements (i) the work places have to be created in areas where the people are living now; (ii) these work places must be, on the average, cheap enough so that they can be created in large numbers without making undue demands on savings and imports, (iii) the production methods employed must be relatively simple so that the demands of high skills are minimised, not only in the production process itself but also in the matters of organization, raw material supply, financing, marketing, and so forth, and (iv) production should be largely for local use.[21]

It follows from foregoing discussions that the right court for India, as Gandhi argued, was to concentrate on generation of employment in the countryside through capital-saving handicrafts and capital-saving agricultural techniques, so that by a multiplier processes increasing output and employment could generate what Myrdal has called the 'Spread-effects' of economic development, as contrasted with its 'backwash effects' the entire process depending, as far as possible, on what Marx described as the 'intimate connection' or identity between local sales and purchases, with the rate of exploitation having been reduced to the minimum.[22]

It has to be admitted the technology cannot be taken to village at one stroke. It is a two way process, rural areas have to prepare themselves to receive it as much as the means and ways have to be found to take modern ideas and techniques to the villages. While approaching the villager, we must always remember that although he may be illiterate in the formal sense, he has wisdom and knowledge derived from long experience and from toiling in the sun and rain. He is close to nature and therefore understands it best. Those who undertake this programme should keep this in mind and go to the villages as seekers of knowledge and as workers in development.

To conclude we can assert that Gandhian philosophies of rural industrialization are not the outmoded concepts of an idealist thinker but are essentially scientific and rational concepts and in tune with modern economic themes regarding the economic growth of developing countries. Thus if the Gandhian ideas are linked up with the broad functioning of our economic planning and the present socio-economic structure is changed on Gandhian lines, were are sure to achieve all round progress and prosperity.

References

1. Journal of Gandhian studies, Vol. 7, 1980, p.188.
2. *Ibid.*, p. 189.
3. *Ibid.*, p.189.

4. *Ibid.*, p.191
5. *Ibid.*, p. 191
6. P.C. Joshi : Gandhi and Econmic and social Development in India. In Research on Gandhian Thought, June 1969, p. 63.
7. Journal of Gandhian Studies, 1980, Vol. 7, 192.
8. *Ibid.*, p. 193.
9. *Ibid.*, p.193.
10. *Ibid.*, p.193.
11. *Ibid.*, p. 194.
12. *Ibid.*, p. 194.
13. *Ibid.*, p. 194.
14. V.S. Sinha : Dynamics of India's Population Growth, p.421.
15. Journal of Gandhian studies, 1980, vol, 7, p. 197.
16. *Ibid.*,.197.
17. *Ibid.*, p. 197.
18. *Ibid.*, p. 197.
19. Gunnar Myrdal ; Asian Drama : An Inquiry into the poverty of Nations, p. 754.
20. D.R. Gadgil : Notes on Rural Industrialization, Artha Vijnana poona.
21. E.F. Schumacher : Small is beautiful, p. 140.
22. B.N. Ganguli : Gandhi's Social Philosphy, p. 302.

7

Relevance of Gandhian Economic Ideas in the Context of Indian Economic Planning

Millions of words have been written on Mahatma Gandhi, his life and works, which offer to scholars a formidable well as fascinating field for research. But the discussion in this chapter will do not more than touching a few basic issues relating to the relevance of Gandhian economic ideas in the context of Indian planning and will try to enquire into the causes of the present, miserable state of affairs of the weaker sections of the population, living particularly in rural areas, in spite of the concerted efforts made under different plans since the very inception of planning in India, adopting the concept of mixed economy, supported by huge plan outlays, modern production technology along with noble objective to initiate "a process of development which will raise the living standards and open out to the people new opportunities for a richer and more varied life".[1] The chapter also intends to make out an inner search into the different plans for the purpose to locate the Gandhian content in Indian economic planning and the position of their implementation with intentions and seriousness of the planners and the executors. Though it seems to be heart pinching to discuss the element of Gandhian economic ideas in Indian planning to make people feel that in Gandhi's own country one will have to try to hard to find even some remote Gandhian elements in Indian planning.

The Existing Socio-Economic Condition

Before having a critical discussion on the different issues relating to relevance of Gandhian ideas in Indian economic planning it would not be out of the way to throw some light on the general background of the strategy and techniques of Indian planning so far adopted for solving the socio-economic problems and the results thereof. It is a fact that India is one of the few countries in the world in which expertise in techniques of planning has been developed to a rather sophisticated extent with all the modern statistical analysis and therefore, one may naturally like to ask the question as to what have been the achievements. It is also a fact that the path followed on the advice of the development model makers has created a modern sector of the economy which has earned us a place among the top ten industrialised nations of the world. But, at the same time, one may ask the question as to why even after the lapse of more than four & half decades of planning, more than 70 per cent of the population is still dependent on agriculture, about 50 per cent of our people are living below the poverty line most of them residing in rural areas, unemployment has increasingly expanded and why we are on top of the world rester of the poor next only to Bangladesh and in spite of the noble objective to raise the living standards of people, the living conditions of people are highly pitiable and shocking? Not only that as Gandhiji feared, the poor, who can least afford, have been made to pay the price for the building up of the modern sector.[2] The presence of socio-economic backwardness, the grindling poverty and distribution, the socio-economic imbalances and inequalities, acute and chronic unemployment and under-employment, mounting debt burden and exploitation of the down trodden is the real outcome of the previous planning efforts in spite of the repeated emphasis of the successive Five Year Plans on these problems as their main objectives. This result is only because, the planners in India have missed the real perspective of the Indian economy and to quote Gunnar Myrdal, "The main reason for slow development in India, is that Indian planners have deviated from the fundamentals of Mahatma Gandhi's rationalistic plans.[3] It is travesty that the land which birth to Gandhi and worships, him is the one that has doggedly followed the path of extorting sacrifices out of the starving poor. After inflicting, thoroughly avoidable, monumental misery on the vast masses the supporters of modern economics now acknowledge the ills of highly capital-intensive technology based on sectoral development planning model so far adopted and if proper corrective measures, in the shape of Gandhian planning is not adopted, the pursuit of investment of current capital-intensity would lead to a far greater mass of humanity being plunged deeper into destitution and unemployment.

The main objective of planning is to mobilise the maximum financial and human resources of a country with a view to securing their best utilisation for the overall development of the country in accordance with certain specified priorities. All economic systems revolve around three problems: production, exchange and distribution and it is only in terms of these that the planning processes are also explained. Planning and policy which ignores the actual connection between and distribution with social justice, growth and resource allocation are unreal. Gandhiji was of the view that "any plan which exploits the raw material of a country and neglects the potentially more powerful manpower is lopsided and can never tend to establish human equality. Real planning consists in the best utilisation of the whole manpower of India and the distribution of the raw products of India in her numerous villages instead of sending them outside and rebuying finished articles at fabulous prices.[4] The results of the Indian Five Year plans indicate that there is something fundamentally lacking in the strategy and process of Indian planning. It may be precisely because in our type of mixed economy "planning is outwardly patterned after the Soviet model but its basic ingredients are those of the Western economics".[5] Those who think that a mixed economy is basically different from the old capitalist mode of production, at least, so far as the rules of profit maximisation, private accumulation and consumer's sovereignty are concerned, are greatly mistaken.[6] The features show that the actual Indian economy of today is no different from the Western mixed economy but the question automatically arises as to why cannot it lead to reduce economic inequality and poverty in the same manner as the Western mixed economies have done? The simple answer is that India's economic environment, particularly the combination of population explosion with acute economic backwardness and resources availability at the very start of the development process, was so vastly different from the Western countries that the same rules which brought there social justice to the masses, failed to deliver the goods in the Indian context.[7] It is unfortunate that our preference for the

Soviet type of planning, within a democratic framework, prevented the planners over the past four and half decades from giving serious attention to the Gandhian concepts which were extremely, relevant to the Indian situation and still they have strong faith in the economic theories, models and approaches and politics as advanced by the Western economists even when they do not have relevance to our problems. Our planners, politicians and most of our economists, being influenced by the West had a blind pursuit and strong fascination with models, equations, sophisticated mathematical and statistical techniques of analysis and always put emphasis on overall rates of growth, to be achieved by a combination of different rates of growth in agriculture, industry and other sectors which resulted in the total neglect of employment as the primary requisite for eliminating mass poverty. Since independence, all those responsible to place only flowers at Gandhi's Samadhi but not faith in his advice and ideas and in the absence of Gandhian approach of planning in Indian conditions, the approach and techniques of economic planning have gone in wrong direction and have not been conducive to create conditions for launching a frontal attack on poverty, unemployment, rural backwardness socio-economic inequalities and imbalances and similar other crucial problems of our economy. Now we have realised the fallacies so far committed which is apparent from the repeated emphasis in plans of the objectives of removal of poverty, unemployment and under-employment, provision of social justice to be achieved in growth and distribution as well as minimisation of the incidence of inequality of wealth and income. But the problem is that still we have not lost the fascination of past theories and models and have not shown any inclination to reject them with open mind even after having realised their uselessness. Though, our planners and politicians have doubts even now in Gandhian way of planning for the solution of the emerging socio-economic problems which is evidence from the fact that they adopt the ideas of Gandhian peacemeal and as a programme in place of giving these items high rank among the basic priorities. But it is time now, when the framework of the Eight Plan is under consideration to look into the economic ideas of Mahatma Gandhi and examine as to how those ideas, if get renewed priority in planning, would be able to provide a better framework for the solution of the problems facing our economy.

The Gandhian Economic Ideas

Gandhiji's vision of the free India was part of a larger vision in which he saw the end of exploitation of the poor by the rich, of the masses by classes of the villages by the towns, of the weaker or so-called under-developed races by the stronger or more advanced one.[8] The economic portion of Gandhi's vision was based on a set of interrelated concepts. Gandhian economics was meant to set up 'Swaraj' or 'Sarvodaya' society characterised by simplicity, self-sufficiency and self-reliance and his 'Swaraj' embodied multi-faceted constructive programmes' and laid heavy emphasis on co-operative and equitable social relations and strove for a renewal and a development of localised economy and village industries and rehabilitation of handicrafts which he felt still essential in any viable solution to the problem of India's enforced poverty.[9] Gandhiji insisted that each village should be economical necessities and as such development of agriculture through decentralisation, self-reliant activities which foster a self-sufficient economy and rural industries constituted the core of Gandhian economics. He believed in 'production by masses' instead of more mass production by machines. He reasoned that this was the only guarantee that a village could remain free and outsiders, fully entitled to the return his labour and not to be robbed of his right and share in the produce. It was also the only viable basis of stable economy, since a system of localised production and distribution would not suffer from the drastic inflations and recessions to which a centralised economy is naturally subjected to. This was the concept of true Swaraj of Gandhiji which in all aspects man-centred, non-exploiting, decentralised simple village economy providing for full-employment to each one of its citizens on the basis of voluntary co-operation.

Gandhiji believed that modern economic systems, rooted as they are in self-indulgence, multiplicity of wants and divorce of ethics from economics are large-scale, mechanised, decentralised, complicated organisation,[10] and they are disfigured by unemployment, under-employment pauperism, exploitation, a mad race for capturing markets and conquering lands for raw materials. Therefore, he had his own indigenous solution to the problem of poverty, inequality and social and economic injustice to be attained by class collaboration, instead of by class conflict and class war. He hoped for and planned for 'a change of heart' to create and environment in which the employer and employee and rich and the poor would work together as one in the service of the nation without exploiting anyone, instead benefiting every one, and in the process be benefited themselves. In this context Gandhiji advocated for the principle of 'trusteeship' whose true implementation was though difficult in practice[11] which he himself felt. But he believed that Indian condition, persuasion or conversion was clearly the better way to coercion or confiscation, which creates ill-will, animosity, wasteful war, instead of increased wealth by common effort, to be shared by agreement in fair proportions. Therefore, he wrote, "I adhere to my doctrine of trusteeship in spite of the ridicule that has been poured upon it. It is true that it is difficult to reach. So is non-violence.".

Gandhi saw the difficulties and dangers of indiscriminate industrialisation in under-developed countries which might result in the concentration of wealth in the hands of a few, or the creation of industrialised urban areas making for lop-sided development and exploitation. Gandhi also advocated that with growing industrialisation the same exploitative relationship between Britain and Indian would come to exist between India's cities and her country side.[12] Mahatma Gandhi was never against industrialisation rather he was against the 'craze' for large scale industrialisation with the help of indiscriminate technological modernisation which may make the reduction of poverty more difficult. Gandhiji knew about his attitude to machinery being much misunderstood. He, therefore, tried to clarify repeatedly his stand thus: 'My opposition to machinery is much, misunderstood, I am opposed to machinery which displaces labour and leaves it idle".[13] He further wrote, "What I object to is the craze for machinery not machinery as such. The craze is for what they call labour-saying machinery".[14] Elimination of mass poverty and unemployment in the shortest possible period was Gandhi's central concern and he believed in giving productive employment rather than 'doles' because, in his ideas "the supreme consideration is man"[15] not economic man of Adam Smith but a man with soul, and ethical values and therefore Gandhiji wrote "that economics is untrue which ignores moral values".[16] He emphasised to organise a network of small, cottage and village industries in the decentralised sector on a very wide basis. Gandhiji foresaw that modernisation would raise per worker capital requirements too rapidly and keep misery on the masses and urbanisation, equal to modern industrialisation, will impose excessive burdens of infrastructure build-up beyond the means of the poor nations. That is why Gandhi was in favour of "Production by masses" in place of the modern craze for "mass production". He realised that the problem of Indian economic development is not merely one of growth but also of rehabilitation and arresting of the growing drift towards urbanisation, a decentralisation of productive activities and an integration of rural and urban economics to ensure orderly production according to needs and therefore, pleaded for a decentralised system of industry on a co-operative basis drawing the frontiers of the common man's world closer to him. This is reason that Prof. G.D.H. Gole, has accepted in 'A Guide to Modern Politics', the Gandhian campaign as a "practical attempt to relieve the poverty and uplift the standards of the Indian villagers".[17]

Confronted with the low level of investible resources, a relatively large increase in the work force and a high capital-intensity of investment and maximise labour intensity where feasible in order to deliver the maximum possible employment to the poor today and not in a distant future which they may not live to see. This does not, however, mean that Gandhiji desired India to go back to the middle ages and patronise outdated technology.[18] Though Gandhiji did not coin the terms, but he was the first to introduce the ideas of appropriate scale and appropriate technology in economics which would help augment agricultural and industrial production for raising the per capita productivity without throwing people out of employment. Certain industries, as Gandhiji viewed, such as steel production and the manufacture of heavy machine tools could not be operated adequately at the local level and therefore, he suggested these to be set up as centralised industries, owned by the Government or by 'trustee' individuals who would manage their enterprises for the benefit of society rather than for personal profit, and operate under Government regulation. Thus, Gandhiji talked of 'Village Swaraj's in which each village was to be largely self-sufficient for its vital requirement and this view is shared now by almost all scientists and economists all over the world. Schumacher went on to add, "ever bigger machines, entailing ever bigger concentrations of economic power and expecting ever greater violence against the environment do not represent progress. They are a denial of wisdom. Wisdom demands a new orientation of science and technology towards the organic, the gentle, the non-violent, the elegant and beautiful".[19] In respect of the solutions of the modern economic problem of the world, Schumacher concluded, "I think, Gandhi has the answer".[20] But unfortunately, Gandhi's views on industrialisation did not comment themselves to the Indian intelligentsia, and even to many of his close associates, scientists, economists, individualists, radicals, socialists, or communists, his economic ideas seemed to throw back to primitiveness to a utopian pre-industrial position which has untenable in the modern world. Through the relevance of Gandhian economic ideas is conceded and appreciated now, but earlier it was condemned either as impractical and utopian or as absolute, anarchronistic and backward looking and Gandhiji was described even by Nehru as a "medievalist in economics". Gandhi analysis has proved true, as it were, with a vengeance because the planning exercise of the past four & half decades with emphasis of large scale industrial development and international trade has increased dramatically the poverty of India's rural population, has induced increasingly unmanageable large-scale migration to the cities and has, in turn, aggravated the problems of unemployment inequality and imbalances in socio-economic development.

Gandhi's entire emphasis was on productive employment, at whatever technological level that was practical, for every able bodied person in the country, especially in the rural areas. His emphasis on Khadi and village industries was intended to emphasise the employment aspect of economic development to well as to relate the promotion of economic activity to meet the basic needs of the population. One of the major defects in Indian planning has been that it has failed in promoting the decentralised production of consumption goods as well as in improving the living conditions of the people. Even now, the decentralised production of basic consumption goods has not received the importance it deserves in our planning with there result that consumption goods have continued to remain scale while their prices have been going up from one plan to another and inflation has been built into Indian planning. The ratio between growth of unproductive jobs in the country to that of productive jobs would make an interesting study and it has been a decisive factor influencing and perpetuating inflation in the economy. Therefore, the battle against this evil has to be fought primarily on production front and the Gandhian concept of 'production by Masses' would prove more fruitful in this direction. This requires some fundamental rethinking to be done regarding the pattern of our planning and the objectives and directions of our fiscal policy.[21] If the benefits of 'Swaraj' have to reach the last man, this can only happen when our development plans are people oriented and not target or expenditure oriented as at present.[22]

One of the prime elements that Gandhiji sought to include in the economic order was economic equality as characterised by the principle of "to each according to his needs. While it might never be possible to achieve total equality in a non-coercive society, it was both possible and necessary to bring the differences within a reasonable range. Central to the concept of economic equality was the idea that all labour has equal value. Ultimately, Gandhiji looked towards an economy built on the principle of "bread labour" that each should perform sufficient manual labour in the production of life's necessities or the equivalent. In the absence of essential physical labour, Gandhiji saw the root of all oppression, exploitation and class division. If the principle of bread labour were followed universally, economic equality and harmonious society would be the natural and inevitable outcome. Such a society, as Gandhiji visioned, on villages politically and economically autonomous, producing a strong self-reliant individuals, would be able to create the basic tenets of 'Swaraj' in all its respects, that was Gandhiji's great dream for India.

Thus, the Gandhian economic ideas, in brief, are attainment of economic equality with the help of non-violent means, end of 'pauperism', idea of 'trusteeship' to be implemented by moral revolution, best utilisation of whole manpower as a key to real planning, village self-sufficiency and self-reliance to be achieved through co-operate activities, adoption of appropriate technology, keeping in mind the labour-absorbing goal in place of labour-saving modernised mechanisation, priority preference to cottage industry for offering full employment and establishing an egalitarian society free of coercion, exploitation to create a self-sufficient and self-reliant society subserving spiritual and moral values. But Gunnar Myrdal holds the view with regret that the social and economic revolution which Gandhiji had thought to be an inevitable accompaniment of independence did not materialise due to the apathy of the destiny makers of post-independence. India towards his plan and the practice of "a certain amount of 'double-talks' in public discussion and tendency to indulge in rhetoric isolated from reality".[23]

Gandhian Contents in Indian Planning"

Keeping in view the above ideas, let us look at the Indian planning practices through different plan periods to see as to what extent plan policies and programmes reflect the Gandhian ideas. So far as the objectives of planning as stated in various plans are concerned, they seem to have incorporated at best some Gandhian elements. Establishment of socialist pattern of society through a reduction in income inequalities and proving additional employment have been the two significant objectives of Indian planning. The idea to consider economic development as a consequence of "intellectual, social and cultural advance"[24] to take up rising standard of life as a means to better intellectual life,[25] "investment in man"[26] the suggestion that "we must discover ourselves fully"[27] and stress on moral, human and spiritual values which give meaning and content to economic progress[28] are fairly the Gandhian contents incorporated in the Indian economic planning. While in the First Plan, "Planning was taken to be purposive adoption of resources to social ends"[29] and the emphasis was put on attaining an economic and social order based on equality to opportunity, social justice, and right to work, the right to an adequate wage and a measure of social security for all citizens,[30] the Second plan stresses "to combine development with reduction in economic and social inequality",[31] the Fourth plan laid emphasis on 'weaker sections' of society and the common man[32] whereas the Fifth[33] and Sixth plans[34] had more broad objectives of attack on mass poverty, inequality and attainment of social and distributive justice and with growth. All these references are sufficient to indicate that in policy formulation of the Indian Plans Gandhian ideas have directly or indirectly influenced the policy makers.

Gandhian concept of economic and social development in terms of village economy with its self-sufficiency has gained significance not only today, but it has run through the Indian plan policies. The C.D. programme, the Crash Programme, Rural Public Works Programme, Village Industries Development Programme, introduction of RIPS, and DICs, Integrated Rural Development Programme, Small Farmer, Marginal Farmer and Agricultural Labour Development Programme, Minimum needs Programme, 20 point Economic Programme, etc. are sufficient to indicate how Gandhian ideas have influenced the policies of the Plans. But these policies and programmes, though have the essence of Gandhian economic ideas have been incorporated in such a planning methodology in Indian which does not suit in existing their results have not been up to expectations. We have though realised the reality and relevance of the Gandhian economic ideas but we have been trying to implement them having the faith in the unrealistic sectoral capital intensive planing without any meaningful changes in our structural and institutional framework. We are turning to Gandhian ideas now not because of objective considerations of those ideas but only because the different alternative approaches have failed to provide meaningful results. In other words, Gandhian elements seem to have been included in the Indian planning processes as a matter of appeasement rather than as a matter of conviction in the Gandhian approach. But the fact is that as Gandhiji was 'a practical idealist' and endeavored to find solutions of different problems facing the country, his ideas are basically sound and relevant to our times. Sriman Narayan, has gone up to the extent to say with conviction that "instead of being medieval and out-of-date, Bapu's ideas are even ahead of times and economic and political compulsions would inevitably force us to revert to them for resolving some of the paradoxes that intrigue us today".[35] Prof. Myrdal also thinks solutions of the Indian socio-economic problems in terms of Gandhian ideas but for its implementation, as he wrote, "the revolutionary changes in social, economic and political institutions, attitude, and practice are separately needed".[36]

To conclude, we can assert that Gandhian ideas of economic development are not the outmoded concepts but are essentially rational and scientific concepts and in tune with modern economic themes regarding economic development of the developing countries like India. Though Gandhiji focussed his attention mostly on the socio-economic problems present in India, but his analysis, vision and strategy bore relevance throughout the globe. But setting aside the world-wide aspect for the movement, even India is apparently no closer to 'Swaraj', than it was while under the British. Yet, on closer examination, we can see that Gandhiji's work has not come to an end. His ideas, so often rejected, misunderstood, and neglected, are finding their way in the consciousness of the world and they are becoming popular and expanding. It is a movement that aims at nothing less than an ultimate transformation of the world-a movement that is not likely to disappear until and unless peace on each becomes a reality.[37] Thus it becomes quite clear that if the Gandhian ideas are linked up with the broad functioning of our economic planning, we are sure to achieve the objectives of our plans.

As our ends are primarily related to eradication of country-wide poverty and unemployment, "our plans must be rooted in the condition that prevail in our land" and must "touch every living person in India"[38] and "provide first the things the village need".[39] This can be possible only by adopting the Gandhian contents in our economic planning. But the success of even Gandhian way of planning is subject of certain conditions. This will require radical changes in the present system of planning and execution. First, planning process should be much from the bottom having the idea of decentralised planning and the plan must consider the needs and circumstances of each family which is below the poverty line. Additional avenues of employment within a reasonable distance must be provided to make full employment a reality. Second the executors or the administrative structure must be able to deliver to every family the basic benefits provided in the plan and participation of people through decentralised people's organisation must be secured in plan formulation and its implementation. Such an approach will need a total reorientation of the present administrative procedure and reorientation of the Panchayats in such a way that they may work as an economic and welfare unit rather than as its present shape being purely involved in political activities. This intends to have people oriented micro-level planning rather than expenditure oriented micro-level sectoral planning with whole hearted support of the plan for the welfare of the masses. Thus, in Gandhian framework, sectoral planning is made subservient to spatial planning and village community becomes the lowest unit of planning. Planned activities from the lowest level upto the national level tend to be interlinked in Gandhian concept and prosperity of the nation. Peoples' participation, co-operation and involvement should essentially be assured and production, distribution and other socio-economic activities should be the integral part of the welfare oriented national plan. In this process, the state has to perform a double role, namely, to plan economic and social development in the interest of the people and also liquidate itself slowly for the same reason so that planning becomes a part of the life of those for whom the planning is designed. If the plan of the country is prepared and implemented in the light of the Gandhian concepts giving appropriate priorities to the sectors relevant for developing the standard of life of the masses along with other allied sectors, the solution of the existing socio-economic problems will come nearer to our approach and the nation along with all its glamorous achievements, will be able to solve the basic problems of poverty, unemployment and inequality in the distribution of income and wealth which was the dream of the 'Father of Nation' for independent India.

References

1. Government of India, Planning Commission, First Five Year Plan, p. 7.
2. Jain, L.C., "Essence and Relevance of Gandhian Economics", Gandhi Marg, July 1980, 230
3. Myrdal, Gunnar, Keynote address while inaugurating the 'One Asia Assembly' in Delhi on 5 February, 1973, quoted in Vaswani, K.N., "Relevance of Gandhian Economic Today" Khadi Gramodyog, January 1979, p. 185.
4. Gandhi, M.K., Harijan 23 March 1947, p. 79.
5. Commerce, August 19, 1972, p. 3.
6. Hajela, P.D., "The Gandhian Technique of Removing Poverty and Inequality", Journal of Gandhian Studies, Allahabad, Vol. II, No. 4 July 1975, p. 235.
7. Ibid, p. 236.
8. Nanda, B.R., "Legacy of Gandhi and Nehru", Gandhi Marg, January 1980, p. 618.
9. Shephard, Mark, "Mahatma Gandhi : The Legacy", Gandhi Marg, April 1980, p. 34.
10. Gandhi, M.K., 'Village Swaraj' (Compiled by H.M. Vyas), Navajivan Publishing House, Ahmedabad, 1962, p. XVI.
11. Gandhi, M.K., Harijan, 3 June 1939, p. 145.
12. Shephard, Mark, op. cit., p. 31.
13. Harijan, 15 September 1946, p. 310.
14. Young India, 13 November 1924, p. 378.
15. Prabhu, R.K. and Rao, U.R., 'The Mind of Mahatma Gandhi," Navajivan Publishing House, Ahmedabad, p. 234.

16. Kripalani, Krishna, 'All Men are Brothers', Navajivan Publishing House, Ahmedabad, p. 166.
17. Cole, G.D.H., quoted in K. Thiagarajan, "Impact of Gandhian Economic on Indian Economic Development", Khadi Gramodyog, March 1977, p. 270.
18. Sriman Narayan, "Sixth Plan : Time for Gandhian Approach", Khadi Gramodyog, July 1977, 431.
19. Schumacher, E.F., 'Small in Beautiful', p. 29.
20. Ibid, p. 34.
21. Narasimham, V.K., "Approaches to India's Economic Problem", Gandhi Marg, March, 1980, p. 79.
22. Patil R.K., "Approaches to India's Economic Problems", Gandhi Marg, March 1983, p. 789.
23. Myrdal, Gunnar, 'Asian Drama', Vol. II, p. 767.
24. First Five Year Plan, p. 11.
25. Second Five Year Plan, p. 24.
26. Third Five Year Plan, p. 19.
27. Draft Fifth Plan, Part I, p. 13.
28. Third Five Year Plan, p. 18.
29. First Five Year Plan, p. 8.
30. Ibid, p. 11.
31. Second Five Year Plan, p. 33.
32. Fourth Five Year Plan, p. 5.
33. Fifth Five Year Plan, p., 7.
34. Sixth Five Year Plan, p. 34.
35. Sriman Narayan, "Relevance of Gandhian Economics", Journal of Gandhian Studies, Allahabad, Vol. No. 17, October 1977, p. 25.
36. Myrdal, Gunnar, "Poverty, Inequality and Gandhi, Journal of Gandhian Studies, Vol. II, No. 4, July 1975.
37. Shephard, Mark, "Mahatma Gandhi : The Legacy', Gandhi Marg, op. cit., p. 38.
38. Kumarappa J.C., 'An Overall Plan for Rural Development', p. 1.
39. Ibid., p. 3.

8
Conclusion

World is today faced with a variety of difficult and intricate problems. The modern military weapons have become so indiscriminate and their effects so catastrophic that the very existence of mankind is threatened Unscrupulous pursuit of material welfare without heading ethical and human values, have eaten into the very vitals of national life and culture. The moral fibre of the people has been weakened. The only practical way to resolve these problems in a lasting manner is to turn once again to the ideals of Mahatma Gandhi study them in depth and find proper solutions for our ailments. Now shadow of doubt can exist that the world needs Gandhiji today more than even before. He is not a relic of the past, but a prophet of the future. In his own words, "so long as my faith burns bright as I hope it will even if I stand alone, I shall be alive in the grave, and what is more, speaking from it". Gandhiji's ideas are by no means outmoded as some believe, and on the contrary might well be applied more often in to-day's world.

The relevance of Gandhian ideas, and their universal applicability is precisely because of the fact that his ideas and thoughts are not based on colonial dominations and exploitative attitudes, cut throat competition, and some other material and worldly values. As against these, they are based on strong human values with moral and spiritual touching. He wanted to give a spiritual touch to all economic, social, political and other problems which he thought as the root cause of all prosperity and happiness. His ideas were always to the best interests and to the real solution of the problem of mankind.

Mahatma Gandhi stood for a simple and, more or less, self-sufficient living in the rural surroundings mainly because he could foresee that a highly sophisticated and centralized life in the cities would inescapably lead to the organisation of in human violences and aggressive nationalism resulting in international tensions and wars of unprecedented devastation. Gandhiji therefore advocated the establishment of ideal villages where the people could pursue the ideal of "Simple living and high thinking".[3] 'Plain living and high thinking'—this ideal is the foundation of Gandhian constructive work. The chief principle of Gandhian economy is simplicity of life. It distinguishes between and high standard of life' and 'a high standard of living '. Simplicity of life means neither poverty nor asceticism. Gandhiji believed in simplicity of living, which does not mean living in poverty as some critics observe. Gandhiji was against pauperism. But this ideal has been criticised, ridiculed and even denounced as an opiate to keep the poor quiet and help the present social order to go on. A continually increasing GNP has become the new God to which both capitalists and communists to obeisance and the sheer number and price of the material goods, one deploys around oneself is taken as the index of one's cultural superiority. But this paradise of free-wheeling euphoria is breaking up. Scientists who have tried to peep into the future have been making gloomy predictions. Two eminent British thinkers, Arnold Toynbee and J.B. Priestly believe that Western civilization, based on the continuous growth of GNP would soon collapse beyond repair, Prof. W.W. Rostow, the author of 'The stages of Economic growth' has revised his thesis and added the last stage for improving ' the quality of life' after the process of' his consumption'. Dr. J.K. Galbraith has been drawing attention to "the public purpose" of economics in his writings. The earth's physical and natural resources and basically limited and indiscriminate use of these resources towards unnecessary and conspicuous consumption will doubtless create scarcity problems for the generation to come. The club of Rome, a forum of the worlds' top economists and scientists has said that there are obvious limits to growth and that mere "growth phobia" will land us in great trouble in the future.

Prof. Dennish Meadows is of the opinion that human environment is a shocking way and there is limit to the world material growth and the world economy faces a very gloomy picture in the coming century if we do not change radically our present policies.

The indiscriminate use of technology and the pursuance of industrialization on competitive basis have led to serve economic and social consequences of new and different nature. The ever widening gap between rich and the poor, worsening economic and political relations, economic imperialism, multinationals and technostructure are among the more important problems at both the internal and international levels, the solution of which is not becoming possible through the traditional and conventional methods of modern world. With reference to these problems the relevance of Gandhian ideas are very much emphasised by Prof. Tinbergin in the following words:- "the rich of the earth should prepare themselves for the simpler life in future. The leading philosophy of the present which asks for more material goods and does not attach much value at simplicity of life or modesty in claims has to be replaced by alternative philosophies and surely much could be learned from Mahatma Gandhi's words and example. The real values of life do contain a sufficient quantity of goods and shelter, but it is not necessary to have the luxuries now aimed at cultural values will have to be upgraded again".[3]

According to Gandhiji advancement, is not only economic or industrial it is the ethical and spiritual progress of man's nobler pursuits for a higher and sublimer and goal of life. Gandhiji says:- "Civilization, in the real sense of the term consists not in the multiplication, but in the deliberate and voluntary reduction of wants. This alone promotes real happiness and contentment and increases the capacity for service".[4] "Our civilization, our culture, our Swaraj (freedom) depends not upon multiplying our wants-self-indulgence, but upon restricting our wants-selfdenial"[5]. Even the laws of diminishing utility and the law of insatiable wants clearly indicate that the more a man has the less he is able to derive pleasure from the articles of consumption .... The end consists in the total elimination of all the wants, existing at the moment". Just a few months before his death Gandhiji wrote to Jawaharlal Nehru: "The new social order that we envisage should not be judged by the quantity of material comfort and luxuries that we are able to accumulate, but by the high standard of moral and ethical values that govern the life of a nation".[6] He advised simplification of the standards of living and that one should place voluntary limits on his property and practise self-renunciation. He held that "many of the so called comforts of life are not only indispensable but positive hindrances to the elevation of mankind".[7]

Having correctly diagnosed the disease, he called for the revival of village economy with indigenous industries so that the people could have enough to eat and keep the wolf off their doors.

Gandhiji favoured "Production by the masses" opposed to "mass production". But it is significant that he never opposed machinery as such:- what he opposed was craze for machinery. Gandhiji was realist: he knew that every country needs certain large-scale industries to cater to vital needs-steel, cement and so on. He knew that even millions of blacksmiths cannot replace a steel plant. But, according to him, such industries should be controlled and managed by the state and should occupy "the least part of the vast national activities which will mainly be in the villages".[8]

Gandhiji's plan of production by the masses also has other distinct advantages over mass production. As Dr. Schumacher wrote, "The system of mass production, based on sophisticated, highly capital-saving technology presupposes that you are already rich, for a great deal of capital investment, is needed to establish one single work place. The system of production by the masses mobilizes the priceless resources which are possessed by all human brings, their clever brains and skilful hands, and supports them with first-class tools. The technology of mass production is inherently violent, ecologically damaging, self-defeating in terms of non-renewable resource, and stultifying for the human person. The technology of mass production by the masses, making use of the best of modern knowledge and experience is conducive to decentralization, compatible with laws of ecology, gentle in its use of scarce resources, and designed to serve the human person instead of making him the servant of machines".[9]

For a moment, let us take it for granted that the total output under mass production is larger than that under the system of production by the masses; even then the latter should be preferred over the former from the view point of distributional aspect. Gandhiji remarked "Granting for the moment that machinery may supply all the needs of humanity, still it would concentrate production in particular areas, so that you have to go in around-about way to regulate distribution both in the respective areas where things are required, it is automatically regulated and there is less chance for fraud, and none for speculation".[10] It is worth noting that vast organisations like the General Motors Corporation of the united states and the British National Coal Board have been decentralized to improve efficiency and promote employee's welfare and job satisfaction.

Gandhiji's views on the social responsibility of business and his trusteeship theory constitute a revolutionary step in the field of socio-economic reform.

Under Trusteeship there is no room for serving the personal interests either of the owners or of the workers alone or even of an enterprise as a whole at the cost of the rest of the society. "Trusteeship presupposes that an enterprise is useful and therefore units which are bareful will have to shut their doors. Voluntary transformation of the socio-economic order is the essence of Trusteeship. Here legislative action, which is not backed by public and if needed by mass action, cannot be an instrument of ushering a new social order. This has been the experience of all nations. Gandhiji's trusteeship formula is not a device to accommodate the owning class, with its shady part and shader current practices, in the frame work of the existing order, but a means of putting an end to that order by transforming the basis of ownership".[11] It is not a coincidence that Gandhiji's trusteeship theory is very akin to the views on the social responsibility of business expressed by western thinkers and businesses today. Organizations like the Rockfeller and Ford foundations are examples of such views in practice. As Gandhiji said "To my mind as a man looks upon himself as servant of society earns for its sake, then his earnings are good and his business venture is constructive".[12]

He also said that "Absolute Trusteeship is an abstraction like Euclid's definition of a point and is equally unattainable. But if we strive for it we shall be able to go further in realising a state of equality on earth than by any other method....".[13]

Absence of peace is both the cause and effect of tensions in the social, national and international spheres. It frustrates all attempts at economic development, social progress and human solidarity. Inspite of several efforts made by League of Nations and U.N.O for co-operation and goodwill in the world, the battles have still been going on and a wave of cold war has swept over the world which has created a suffocating atmosphere. No where is peace found. The race for armament is still going on. The U.N.O. recognizes that the government of almost all the countries of the world are not prepared to renounce war for one reason or the other. War cannot produce peace. It produce only war. One cannot expect peace from the balance of power since it nourishes mutual hatred, struggle for widening the sphere of influence fear and suspicion which may be the elements of generating wars. Hence some new and basic thought will have to be adopted for permanent and long-lasting world peace.

Gandhi an apostle of non-violent action never approved war-a violent action. He rejected outright and condemned war as a means of resolving a conflict. According to Gandhiji the problem of peace was not just a political problem involving the adjustment or rectification of relations between armed nations. It was the problem of mankind, posing a challenge not only to states but also to every individual human being and human group. He, therefore, endevoured to establish peace between man and man, group and group and nation and nation.

It was a life conviction with Gandhiji and making and its, civilization can be saved from destruction only through non-violence. The individual as well as his environment-local, national and international have to purged of violence. If the individual regenerates himself through strict self-discipline, and if the nations of the world reconstruct themselves along non-violent lines, the emerging international order will naturally be peaceful and co-operative. The great fear of a war and destruction could at once disappear. Indeed the adoption and practice of such an idea at global level is an urgent need of the day.

Gandhiji conceived and wished the development of our society on the lines of Ram Rajya, where every one enjoyed life full of happiness and devoid of any ailment-physical or otherwise. He thought of a society where every one had equal opportunity to develop equal rights and benefits, as far as possible. He advocated simple life with austerity but with noble thoughts not thinking of "self" alone but sacrificing the 'self' for the sake of others. He thought of a society which was self-sufficient economy and where all the necessaries were provided to all and sundry. He took a village, the nerve centre of the country, to be as a unit for the purpose of development and wanted it to be self-sufficient as far as possible. He wanted us all to practise all the virtues, which may be briefly summed up in two virtues i.e., truth and non-violence and shun all which we have branded as sins' from time to time. He wanted to pursue the truth and non-violence with encouragement and conviction in the broadest sense of the terms. For this, he wanted each of us to leave our cowardish mentality and be courageous enough to face the challenges of life boldly. He thought of a society where men and women live together with equal rights without any distinction of class, caste or creed and where women were not exploited mainly because they were weak.

a) Have we ever thought to develop our society on those lines?

b) Are we really moving in that direction?

c) Are we thinking on those lines and trying to help the masses?

d) Are our leader or rulers leading us in that direction?

e) Do we have equality of opportunity available to all the countrymen?

f) Are the rich class of the society or business following the concept of trusteeship in practice?

g) Do we find morality, virtues, good values etc., being practised by us and are they reigning supreme over the vices and sins ?

h) Do we have that kind of economic thinking or policies as were advocated by Gandhiji which would have been most beneficial for the teeming masses. Living in poverty?

If we think deeply and at the socio-economic structure of our society we would, in fact not get the answers to the above questions in the affirmative. Changes in socio-economic structure of our country since four and half decades are not in those directions as visualised or advocated by Gandhiji.

We find today, as in the past, duality in the socio-economic structure of our country. On the one hand, we have an affluent class which is living luxuriously and trying to follow the western way of life. The rich of the country have, undoubtedly become richer. On the other hand we have a middle class in our society, struggling for their existence. But in this class also one group has started flourishing, considerably as they are amazing black money losing all their moral values and trying to initiate the rich class of the society. However, the facilities available to lower middle fixed income group have been reduced. Corruption in the society is not only rampant but has become part of life. The poor are becoming poorer and their sufferings have increased considerably. The social structures have not changed on the lines which Gandhiji had thought out. As the policy of the Government planners and the administrators is not going to change considerably in the near future, the prospects of change on Gandhian lines are also quite bleak.

The story of the rural areas is similar, here we cannot deny that any change has taken place. Changes are rather, slower and not visible. Violence, insecurity of life, personal feuds, bickering among themselves, gap between the rich and poor farmers etc.; have increased considerably. The number of persons living below poverty line, has also increased considerably, in view of this, the prospects of changes in rural areas of the country on Gandhian lines are quite bleak.

Gandhiji fought against untouchability, casteism, drinking and other social evils in his life time and showed the ways in which such problems can really be solved. However, even after more than four and half decades, the situation has not improved. Every now and then we listen of exploitation of Scheduled Caste and backward class people. We have still got reservation for them in many areas. Prohibition has not been successful and number of persons, who drink; has been increasing year after year. Communal harmony at the alter of which he scarified his life, is still a dream. Today, we find that communal disturbances have been taking place in the country now and then. From this point of view also change as desired by Gandhiji has not taken place.

We find the impact of hippy cult, jeans, pop culture, disco, five star culture etc.: on the minds of the youth of the country. Those who are educated find themselves completely alienated from the common man. We have become more and more materialistic in our approach and we are multiplying our wants day-by-day. The idea of self-sacrifice or wantlessness or say minimisation of wants is not the talk of the day in the society. One basic premise which Gandhiji enunciated was the need for restriction of wants. He pointed out that we are not always aware of our real needs and most of us improperly multiply our wants and thus unconsciously, make thieves of ourselves". There is not doubt that since Gandhiji's time the craze for material goods has intensified and India too has been infected with it. This produces visible disparities between the rich and the poor and leads to social discord between the two". In this connection, we can quote Sir Julian Huxley, who pointed out that "Like population explosion, the consumption explosion cannot continue much longer; it is an inherently self-defeating process. Sooner, rather than later, we shall be forced to get away from a system based on artificially increasing the number of human wants and set about constructing one aimed at the qualitative satisfaction of real human needs spiritual and mental, as well as material and psychological".[15] But what we find today is that there is a mad race for more and more goods not only in the urban areas but also in the rural areas.

So far as economic structure of the society is concerned we are no where near the drams of Gandhiji. Majority of our country men ridicule economic thinking of Gandhiji and feel that if we would follow his economic ideas the country would go back to the barbaroud age and the progress would be stopped. We would continue to remain poor and the world would simply laugh at us. We brand him old fashioned. But we forget that Gandhi was more pragmatic, more close to the reality and he new the country and countrymen very well. The solutions which he provided for the amelioration of the economic lot of the masses are highly practical and relevant, even though it is not based on technologically based industrialisation that encourages mad race for materialistic development. We forget that even though Gandhiji spoke in the traditional language but the content of his programmes was radical and that a man who combined wisdom with an intuitive knowledge of the country.

Economic ideas of Gandhiji regarding the system of planning, production, methods of management, involvement of the workers, the role of the owners etc.; are highly radical and require a serious thinking on our part. What we have adopted is the centralised system of planning, heavy reliance upon highly technical, capital-oriented heavy industrial growth increased role of state in the economic activities etc.; which are not close to the thinking of Gandhiji. The Community Development Schemes run by the Government half-heartedly, the Bhoodan movement initiated by Sri. Vinoba Bhave, the Panchayat Raj system all have achieved only limited success or it would be better to say that such noble schemes have almost failed to click to bring about desired achievement in the country. The type of economic development which we have been able to achieve and the way we have achieved it and the result which we have attained are eye-openers. Even after about four and half decades of planned development we find that about half of the country live below the poverty line and unemployment is rampant. Use of village industries products has not increased and with that the main source of occupation providing employment to millions is also dwindling. The craze for foreign goods is again on the increases. Use of simpler technologies for production, decentralised system of production providing more and more employment opportunities, development of self-reliant villages or integrated planned development of all the areas of the country are still not given proper attention. Even the minimum needs of our countrymen have not been fulfilled. The planners simply give lip-service to these vital aspects of development. Gunnar Myrdal has rightly realised that "Gandhiji was certainly a planner and his approaches for the development of this country are quite right. He once stated that Mohan Das Gandhi was adamant in stressing the human factor in economic development. To him development meant that people every where in the country and not least in the villages where most of the people live, were brought to bring to act more rationally and effectively and that they then changed their society to make this more possible. Gandhiji was certainly a planner and a rationalistic planner but his planning was all embracing".[16] He further stated that "It is only in the latest years that we have generally come back to Gandhiji's ideas. Some economists have been pressing for an integrated planning". Which is the modern term for what Gandhi was all the time teaching. The main reason why planning in India did not prove more successful is that they have not keep so close, as they should, to the fundamentals of the teachings of the Father of the Nation".[17] We are more enamoured by the system of planing and models of growth of the Western Countries and have not given due attention to what Gandhiji said. Gandhian planning is essentially democratic and humanistic in essence. It is humanistic because its first postulate is to provide employment to all. It is democratic because the fruits of labour and capital are to be shared by all and for the welfare of all. This is the essence of sarvodaya which still remains an idealized goal of Gandhian Thought.

It is interesting to note that the concept of trusteeship to which

Gandhiji laid emphasis has not been practised at all in this country where as we find a few instances in other countries of the world? His doctrine of trusteeship has been regarded as naive and unrealistic and the critics have denounced it as hypocritical or even a camouflage. It is have been rightly stated that, "It is some what ironic that in the land of his own birth where for nearly four and half decades Gandhi was struggled and demonstrated, there is hardly any industrial organization which has attempted to put his ideas sincerely into practice. This is indeed a challenge to India and to all those who believe in the strength of principles which he had preached so incessantly during his life time".[18]

We are after the introduction of the most modern and sophisticated technology so that we may be able to march with out heads high among the top ranking countries of the world. What have were achieved by adopting them is not unknown to us. We did not bother about adoption of simpler technology and feel that they are backward and second grade. We forget that it does not imply backward or second grade.

In retrospect, one cannot fail to agree with Louis Fischer who wrote "If man is to survive, if civilization is to survive and flower in freedom, truth and democracy the remainder of the twentieth, century and what lies beyond must belong not to Lenin or Trotsky nor to Marx or to Mas or Ho or Che, but to Mahatma Gandhi".[20]

No one has ever suggested that grailing poverty can lead to anything else than moral degradation? The Wealth of the nation lies in happy and healthy people, not in terms of gold, silver or power. If human power is properly challenged for constructive purposes, India with her huge man-power will one day become the most prosperous and developed nation. At present a vast reserve of human skills and energises, is going to waste. With a little more encouragement, and proper direction by the government, there energies could provide a dynamic force for India's national development.

Problems in regard to decentralized system of production restriction on wants, proper distribution, industrialism, mechanization of man, minimum wage, role of trade unionism, economic equality, relationship with land lord and peasant, capital and labour and other allied economic problems-all these find a solution in the all comprehensive Gandhian principles of economics, viz., Sarvodaya which aims at the welfare of all.

Therefore we can conclude that Gandhian economic thought may be described as *Pragmatic humanistic economy* because it is based on realistic approach to life with emphasis on human value and human dignity.

If we are able to live according to the ideals of Mahatma Gandhi, we may be sure that this country of ours will survive, as it has survived for centuries, for many more centuries and its philosophy will make a healing of nations and bringing of people together.

"asato mā sad gamaya
tamaso mā jyotir gamaya
mrtyor mā amrtama gamaya".

Lead me from the unreal to the real
Lead me from darkness to light
Lead me from death to eternal life.

May the life and teachings of Mahatma Gandhi be a beacon of hope and courage to all of us.

References

1. Paul F. power, Gandhi on World Affaris.
2. Shriman Narayan, Principles of Gandhian Planning.
3. Jan Tinbergin, Limit to Growth, The Economic Times, Annual, 1972.
4. J.S. Mathur (ed.) Economic Thought of Mahatma Gandh.p.612.
5. J.S. Mathur(ed.) Economic Thought of Mahatma Gandhi, p. 527.
6. International Newsletter on peace Research (Ann Arbon) Vol. I, No. 3, p.3.
7. Young India, Jan. 14 (1932).
8. Journal of Peace Research (1969), pp. 170-171.
9. Journal of Gandhian studies (January 1982) p.104.
10. Ibid.
11. Pyarelal, Gandhian thought and contemporary soceity, p.30.
12. Mahatma Gandhi, The Doctrine of the Sword 1920.
13. M.K. Gandhi, Trusteeship, Series 13, p.12.

14. Journal of Gandhian studies (July 1981) p. 254.
15. Ibid.
16. Journal of Gandhian studies 1981, p.287.
17. Journal of Gandhian Studies 1981, p. 258.
18. Ibid.
19. T.K.N. Unnithan and Y.Singh, Tradition of Non-violence, New Delhi, 1973, pp. 53-54.

Bibliography

Agarwal, S.N., *Gandhian Constitution for free India*, Kitabistan, (Allahabad, 1946).

Aiyangar, K.VR., *Some Aspects of Ancient Indian Policy*, (Madras, 1935).

Aiyar, S.R., *Modernization of Traditional Society and other Essays*, Macmillan, (Delhi, 1973).

Alexandar, Harace., *Social and Political Ideas of Mahatma Gandhi*, (New Delhi, 1949).

Andrews, C.F., *Mahatma Gandhi's Ideas*, (New York, 1930).

Anstey, Vera., *The Economic Development of India*, Longmans Green & Co., 1946.

Appa Saheb Patwardhan., *Towards a New Society.*, A.B.S.S.S. (Varanasi, 1959).

Bandoyopodhya, N.C., *Development of Hindu Polity and Political Theories*, (Calcutta, 1927).

Barker, Ernest., *Principles of Social and Political Theory*, Oxford University Press, (London, 1965).

Behari, Bepin., *Gandhian Economic Philosophy*, Vora & Co., (Bombay, 1963).

Belshaw, C.E., *Traditional Exchange and Modern Markets*, (New Jersy, :Englewood Cliffts, Prentice-Hall, Inc. 1965).

Benn, S.I. and Peters, R.S. *Social Principles and the Democratic State*,

George Allen & Unvin Ltd., (London, 1958).

Bhave, Acharya Vinoba., *Democratic Values*, S.S.S. (Varanasi, 1962).

Bhave, Acharya Vinoba., *From Bhoodan to Gramdan* S.P. (Tanjore, 1967).

Bhave, Acharya Vinoba., *Gramdan - villagism of Land*, S.P. (Tanjore, 1968).

Bhave, Acharya Vinoba., *Sarvodaya and Communism*, S.P. (Tanjore, 1957).

Bilpondiwala, Nosir., *The Social Order and Sarvodaya*, S.S.S. (Varanasi, 1963).

Black, C.E., *The Dynamics of Modernization*, Harper & Row, (New York, 1967).

Bluntscli, J.C., *Theory of the State*, English Translation, Second Edition, (Oxford, 1892).

Bondurant, J.V., Conquest of Violence : *The Gandhian Philosophy of Conflict*, Princeton University Press, (Princeton, J.N. 1958).

Bonsanquet, Bernard., *The Philosophical Theory of the State*, Macmillan & Co., Ltd., (London, 1958).

Bose, N.K., *Selections from Gandhi*, N.P.H. (Ahmedabad, 1948).

Bose, N.K., *Studies in Gandhism*, Merit Publisher, (Calcutta, 1962).

Bradley, F.N. *Ethical Studies*, (Bombay, 1876).

Buch, M.A., *The Development of Contemporary Indian Political Thought*, Good Companions, (Baroda, 1939, Vols. I, II & III).

Buch, M.A., *Rise and Growth of Indian Nationalism*, (Baroda, 1939).

Carus, D.P., *The Nature of the State*. The Open Court Publishing Company, (Chicago, 1894).

Catlin, George., *In the Path of Mahatma Gandhi*, (Chicago, 1950).

Chakravarthy, Amia., *Mahatma Gandhi and the Modern World*, Book House, (Calcutta, 1945).

Char, Narasimha: *A Day Book of Thoughts from Mahatma Gandhi*, (Macmillan, 1969).

Chari, C.T.K., *Some Issues about Social Change*, (University of Madras, 1973).

Chatterjee, B.B., *Gramdan and People*, (S.S.S.P. Varanasi, 1969).

Cahattopathyay Kamala Devi., *Mahatma Gandhi 100 Years*, Gandhi Peace Foundation, (New Delhi 1969).

Cobban, Alfred., *Rousseau and the Modern State*, (London, 1934).

Coleman, James, S., *Modernization: Political Aspects*, International Encyclopaedia of the Social Science, Vol.10, David L. Sills (Editor) The Macmillan Company and the Free Press, (New York, 1968).

Cooley, C.H., *Human Nature and the Social Order*, Charless Seribner's Sons, (New York, 1922).

Datta Bhabatosh., *Indian Economic Thought*, Tata Macgraw, New Delhi, 1978).

Datta, D.M., *The Philosophy of Mahatma Gandhi*, The University of Wisconsin Press, (Madison, 1953).

Davies, Kingsley., *Human Society*, The Macmillan Company, (New York, 1970).

Daya Krishna., *Social Philosophy - Past and Future*, Indian Institute for Advanced Study, (Simla, 1968).

Dayananda., *Light of Truth*, (Allahabad, 1915).

Deininger, Whitaker, T., *Problems in Social and Political Thought*, Macmillan, (London, 1965).

Desai, Mahadev., *Gandhi in Indian Villages*, Navajivan, (Ahmedabad).

Desai, Mahadev., *The Gita according to Gandhi.*

Devanesan, Chandran.D.S., *The Making of the Mahatma*, Oriental Longmans, (Madras, 1969).

Devadoss, T.S., *Sarvodaya and the Problem of Political Sovereighty*, University of Madras, (Madras, 1974).

Dhawan, Gopinath., *The Political Philosophy of Mahatma Gandhi*, N.P.H., (Ahmedabad, 1951).

Diwakar, R.R., *Mahatma Gandhi 100 Years*, Gandhi Peace Foundation, (New Delhi, 1968).

Fischer, Louis., *Gandhi : His life and Message for the World*, (New York, 1954).

Fisher, Louis, *The Life of Mahatma Gandhi*, Jonathan Cape., (London, 1951).

Gandhi, Indira., *The Years of Challenge*, Publications Division, (New Delhi, 1973).

Gandhi, Kanu., *Swaraj Through Charkha*, (Sevegram, 1945).

Gandhi, M.K., *Basic Education* N.P.H. (Ahmedabad, 1951).

Gandhi, M.K., *Communal Unity*, N.P.H. (Ahmedabad, 1949).

Gandhi, M.K., *Constructive Programme: Its meaning and place*, (Ahmedabad, Navajivan Press, 1944).

Gandhi M.K., *Constructive Programme*, N.P.H., (Ahmedabad, 1945).

Gandhi, M.K., *Economic and Industrial Life and Relations*, Vol, I, II & III, N.P.H., (Ahmedabad, 1858).

Gandhi, M.K., *Economics of Khadi*, N.P.H., (Ahmedabad, 1941).

Gandhi M.K., *Ethical Religion*, S. Ganeshan, (Madras, 1922).

Gandhi, M.K., *Hind Swaraj or Indian Home Rule*, N.P.H., (Ahmedabad, 1939).

Gandhi. M.K., *Harijan.*

Gandhi M.K., *India of My Dreams*, N.P.H. (Ahmedabad, 1958).

Gandhi., M.K., *In Search of the Supreme*, N.P.H., (Ahmedabad, 1951).

Gandhi, M.K., *Non-violence in Peace and War*, N.P.H., Part I & II, (Ahmedabad, 1945).

Gandhi, M.K., *Rebuilding our Villages*, N.P.H., (Ahmedabad, 1952).

Gregg, R.B., *A Philosophy of Economic Development*, N.P.H. (Ahmedabad).

Gregg, Richard, B., *A Philosophy of Indian Economic Development*, N.P.H., (Ahmedabad, 1958).

Gupta, Shanti, S., *The Economic Philosophy of Mahatma Gandhi*, Ashok Publishing House, (New Delhi).

Hegel, G.W.F., *The Philosophy of Right*, Translated by S.W. Dyde, (London, 1896).

Heimsath, Charles, H., *Indian Nationalism and Hindu Social Reform*, Princeton, (New Jersey, 1964).

Horace, Alexander and Others., *Social and Political ideas of Mahatma Gandhi.*

Hunt, Elgin, F., *Social Science*, Macmillan, (New York, 1972).

Inkeles, Alex., *Becoming Modern*, Paper Presented at Michigan State University, 1967).

Kalekar Kaka., *To a Gandhian Capitalist*, A.P.H. (Bombay, 1951).

Karan Singh., *Prophet of Indian Nationalism*, George Allen & Unwin Ltd., (London, 1963).

Kela Bhagavan Das., *Bhoodan, Shramdan, Jeevandan, Bharatiya Grandhamala*, (Allahabad, 1955).

Kumarappa, Bharatan., *Capitalism, Socialism or Villagism?* S.S.S. (Varanasi, 1965).

Kumarappa, Bharatan: *Sarvodaya*, Ahmedabad, N.P.H. 1958.

Kripalani, J.B., *Gandhian Thought*, Orient Longmans, (Calcutta, 1961).

Kripalani, J.B., *Toward Sarvodaya*, Kisan Mazdoor Praja Party, (New Delhi, 1951).

Kumarappa, J.C., *Economy of Permanence*, S.S.S., (Varanasi, 1958).

Kumarappa., J.C., *Gandhian Economic Thought*, S.S.S. (Varanasi, 1962).

Gandhi, M.K., *Sarvodaya*, N.P.H., (Ahmedabad, 1951).

Gandhi, M.K., *Styagraha*, N.P.H., (Ahmedabad, 1951).

Gandhi, M.K., *Towards New Education*, N.P.H., (Ahmedabad).

Gandhi, M.K., *Towards Non-Violent Socialism*, N.P.H. (Ahmedabad, 1951).

Gandhi, M.K.,.....*Unto this Last*, N.P.H., (Ahmedabad, 1951).

Gandhi, M.K., *Village Swaraj*, N.P.H. (Ahmedabad).

Gandhi, M.K. *Varnashrama Dharma*, N.P.H., (Ahmedabad, 1962).

Ganguli, B.N., *Gandhi's Social Philosophy*, Vikas Publishing House (P) Ltd., (Delhi, 1973).

Ganguli, B.N., *Indian Economic Thought*: Nineteenth Century Perspective, New Delhi, Tata McGraw-Hill Publishing Co. Ltd., 1977).

Gandhi, B.N., *Readings in Indian Economic History*, A.P.H., (Bombay, 1964).

Glyn Richard., *The Philosophy of Gandhi*, Barnes & Noble Books (1982).

Kumarappa, J.C., *Gandhian Way to Life*, A.I.V.I.A., (Wardha, 1949).

Kumarappa, J.C., *Swaraj for the Masses*, S.S.S., (Varanasi, 1957).

Kumarappa, J.C., *The Non-violent Economy and World Peace*, S.S.S. (Varanasi, 1958).

Kumarappa, J.C., *Why the Village Movement?* A.I.V.I.A., (Wardha, 1949).

Lanza Del Vasto, J.J., *Gandhi to Vinoba*, Rider, (London, 1956).

Lerner, Daniel, *The Passing of Traditional Society*, The Free Press of Glencoe, (Illinois, 1958).

Maciver, R.M., *The Modern State*, Oxford Univesity Prèss, (London, 1966).,

Mackenzie Brown., *Traditions of Leadership and Political Institutions in India*, Princeton, (New Jersey, 1959).

Mahadevan, T.M.P. *Outlines of Hinduism*, Chetana Limited, (Bombay, 1960).

Manshardt, Cifford (Ed.): *The Mahatma and the Missionary*, Chicago, 1949.

Mathur, J.S. & Mathur, A.S., *Economic Thought of Mahatma Gandhi*, Caitanya Publishing House, (Allahabad, 1962).

Mathur, J.S., *Industrial Civilization and Gandhian Economics*, Pustakaya, (Allahabad, 1971).

Mehta, V., *Social Theory and Political Thought of Sarvodaya*, Laski Institute, (Ahmedabad).

Mehta, V.L., *Decentralised Economic Development*, Khadi & Village Industries Compilation, (Bombay, 1964).

Merton, R., *Social Theory and Social Structure*, Free Press, (Gencoe, 1947).

Misra, B.R., *Vinoba: the Economics of Bhoodan Movement*, Orient Longmans, (Calcutta, 1956).

Misra, R.N., *Bhoodan Movement in India*, S.Chand & Co., (New Delhi, 1972).

Motwani, Kewal., *Manu: a study in Hindu Social Theory*, Ganesh and Company, (Madras, (India) 1934).

Moore, Wilbert, E., *Social Change*, Princce-Hall of India, Second Edition, (New Delhi, 1975).

Mukerji, B., *Community Development in India*, Orient Longmans, (Bombay, 1961).

Mukerjee, Hireu., *Gandhi, A Study*, (Peoples Publishing House, 1960).

(Mukerjee, Rudha Kamal, *The Social Structure of Values*, Macmillan & Co., (London, 1949).

Murthy, R.H., *The Individual and the State*, Hutchinson & Co., Ltd., (London, 1926).

Myrdal, Gunnar., *Economic Theory and Underdeveloped Regions*, (London 1961).

Nagaraja Rao, P., *Contemporary Indian Philosophy*, B.V.B., (Bombay, 1971).

Nag, Kalidas., *Tolstoy and Gandhi*, Pustak Bhandar, (Patna, 1950).

Narayan, Jayaprakash., *From Socialism to Sarvodaya*, S.S.S.P., (Varanasi, 1959).

Narayan, Jayaprakash., *Fundamental Problems of Panchayat Raj*, All India Panchayat Parishad, (New Delhi, 1964).

Narayan, Jayaprakash., *Socialism, Sargvodaya and Democracy*, A.P.H., (Bombay, 1964).

Narayan, Jayaprakash., *Gandhi, Vinoba and the Bhudan Movement*, S.S.S. P., (Varanasi, 1959).

Narayan, Jayaprakash., *Swaraj for the people*, S.S.S., (Varanasi, 1961).

Narayan, Shriman., *Principles of Gandhian Planning*, Kitab Mahal, (Allahabad, 1960).

Narayan, Shriman., *Relevance of Gandhian Economics*, N.P.H., (Ahmedabad, 1970).

Nehru, Jawaharlal., *Mahatma Gandhi*, A.P.H., (New Delhi, 1949).

Nikam, N.A., *Gandhiji's Discovery of Religion*, B.V.B., (Bombay, 1963).

Nye, F.I., *Values., Family and Changing Society*, 1967.

Ommen, T.K., *Chrismatic Movements and Social Change: An Analysis of Bhoodan-Gramdan Movement in India*, University of Poona, (Poona, 1967).

Parsons Talcott., *Structure and Process in Modern Societies*, Free Press of Glencoe, (New York Inc., 1959).

Parsons Talcott., *The Social System*, The Free Press, (Glencoe, 1951).

Prasad, Bimla (Ed.)., *Socialism, Sarvodaya and Democracy*, Selected works of N.P. Narayanan, A.P.H., (New Delhi, 1964).

Pyarelal., *Gandhian Techniques in the Modern World*, N.P.H., (Ahmedabad, 1959).

Pyarelal., *Mahatma Gandhi: The Early Phase*, 2 Vol., N.P.H. (Ahmedabad, 1966).

Pyarelal., *Mahatma Gandhi: The Last Phase*, 2 Vols., N.P.H. (Ahmedabad, 1959).

Radhakrishnan, S., *An Idealist View of Life*, George Allen & Unwin Ltd., (London, 1952).

Radhakrishanan, S., *Freedom and Culture*, G.A. Natesan & Co., (Madras, 1936).

Radhakrishnan, S., *Religion and Society*, Geroge Allen & Unwin Ltd., (London, 1956).

Radhakrishnan, S., *The Hindu View of Life*, George Allen & Unwin Ltd., 1949.

Radhkrishnan, S., *Mahatma Gandhi, Essays and Reflections*, Jaico Publishing House, (Bombay, 1956).

Ranadive, B.T., *Sarvodaya and Communism*, Party Publication, (New Delhi, 1958).

Rao, V.K.R.V., *Gandhian Alternative to Western Socialism*, B.V.B., (Bombay, 1971).

Ray, Benoy Gopal., *Gandhian Ethics*, Navajivan, 1950.

Reddy, V. Narayan Karan., *Sarvodaya ideology and Acharya Vinoba Bhave*, A.P. Sarvodaya Mandal, (Hyderabad, 1963).

Rolland Romain., *Mahatma Gandhi*, (New York, 1924).

Ropkem, Wilhelm., *Humane Economy*, (Londo, 1961).

Ruskin, J., *Unto this Last*, Smith, Elder, (London, 1962).

Russell, Bertrand., *The Prospects of Industrial Civilization*, George Allen & Unwin, (London, 1959), II Edition.

Saiyidain, K.G., *Significance of Gandhi as a man and thinker*, P.D., (New Delhi, 1970).

Santhanam, K., *Satyagraha and the State*, A.P.H. (Bombay, 1960).

Schumacher, E.F., *Roots of Economic Growth*, The Gandhian Institute of Studies, 1962.

Schumacher, E.F., *Small is beautiful* (1975), Abucus, Sphere Book Ltd., London.

Sen, Mankumar., *Gandhian Way and the Bhoodan Movement*, S.S.S., (Varanasi, 1964).

Sen, M.(ed)., *The Economic Aspects of Sarvodaya*, Proceedings of the Calcutta Seminar, S.S.S.P. (Varanasi, 1959).

Shukla, C., *Gandhi's View of Life*, B.V.B., (Bombay, 1951).

Sitaramayya, B.P., *Gandhi and Gandhism*, Vols. I, II, Kitabistan, (Allahabad).

Tagore, Rabindranath., *Nationalism*, Macmillan & Co., (London, 1950).

Tondon Viswanath., *Sarvodaya after Gandhi*, S.S.S. (Varanasi, 1965).

Tendulkar, D.G., *Gandhiji-His Life and Work*, (Bombay, 1944).

Varma, V.P., *Hindu Political and Thought*, Lakshmi Narain Agarwal, (Agra, 1959).

Verma, V.P., *The Political Philosophy of Mahatma Gandhi and Sarvodaya*, Lakshmi Narain Agarwal, (Agra, 1959).

Weiner, Myron (ed)., *Modernization: The Dynamics of Growth*, Voice of America Forum Lectures, Study Circle Reprints, Higginbothams (P) Ltd., (Madras, 1967).

Weldon, T.D., *States and Morals: A Study in Political Conflicts*, (London, 1946).

Wellock, Wilfred., *Gandhi as Social Revolutionary*, Orchard Lea, (New Longton, Preston, England).

Willoughby., *The Ethical Basis of Political Authority*, The Macmillan Company, (New York, 1930).

S. Ganeshan., *Young India*, (Madras, 1919-1922, 1924-1926, 1927-1928), Vols., I, II & III.

Zaehner, R.C., *Hinduism*, Oxford University Press, (1962).

Index